Excel
Basic Skills

Grammar and Punctuation

5–6 Years
Ages 10-12

Get the Results You Want!

Peter Clutterbuck

Reprinted 1999, 2000, 2001, 2003, 2004, 2005, 2006, 2007, 2008, 2009, 2010, 2011, 2012, 2013, 2014, 2017 (twice), 2020, 2022, 2023

ISBN 978 1 86441 285 7

Pascal Press
PO Box 250
Glebe NSW 2037
(02) 9198 1748
www.pascalpress.com.au

Publisher: Vivienne Joannou
Typeset by Grizzly Graphics (Leanne Richters)
Cover by Dizign Pty Ltd
Printed by Vivar Printing/Green Giant Press

About this book

Excel Basic Skills Workbooks are designed not only to help children improve their language skills, but also to widen their knowledge of words.

The activities are simple and self-explanatory, allowing children to work independently within any particular area where they are experiencing difficulty. Answers are provided in a removable answer section.

This book contains all the elements of grammar and punctuation relevant to children aged from 10 to 12. Parents and teachers will not only be able to direct children to specific activities for which there is a need, but will also obtain ideas for further activities to strengthen and reinforce needed skills.

CONTENTS

Year 5

Year 6

A noun is a *naming word*. It can be used to name a person, place, thing or feeling.

Example

Which word best fills the gap?

An ____________ is a type of vegetable.

(a) camera (b) onion (c) elephant

Answer = (b). An ***onion*** *is a type of vegetable.*

Now choose the noun that best fills each space.

1. An ____________ is a large bird.
(a) apple (b) octopus (c) eagle

2. A person who makes bread is a ____________.
(a) baker (b) doctor (c) leader

3. The home of a horse is called a ____________.
(a) web (b) box (c) stable

4. A ____________ is a baby cat.
(a) puppy (b) paper (c) kitten

5. You wear a ____________ on your foot.
(a) glove (b) shoe (c) hat

6. A ____________ has feathers.
(a) bird (b) book (c) bike

7. A ____________ is black and white.
(a) zebra (b) table (c) banana

8. You can see wild animals at a ____________.
(a) school (b) church (c) zoo

9. Circle the nouns in the following passage.

It was a Saturday morning, and after breakfast Tim, Ian and Katy grabbed their hats, put on their trainers and headed down to the creek. They took with them two buckets, three oranges and a small net. Their school was having a science week competition, and they wanted to raise tadpoles till they were fully grown frogs and then release them. They came over the hill, laughing and talking, only to see something that made them stop straight away. There, down by the creek, armed with nets and buckets, were at least ten of the other kids from school, catching all the tadpoles in Farmer's Creek.

UNIT 2 THE FAMILY OF NAMING WORDS YEAR 5
COLLECTIVE NOUNS

Some nouns are used to name groups of people or things. These are called collective nouns.

Which word best fills the gap?
I saw a ____________ of seagulls.
(a) pile (b) flock (c) set
Answer = (b). I saw a ***flock*** *of seagulls.*

Choose the best word to fill the gap.

1. Alice was chased by a ____________ of insects.
(a) flock (b) swarm (c) fleet

2. A ____________ of cattle is on the road.
(a) herd (b) carton (c) tribe

3. The hen has a ____________ of chickens.
(a) brood (b) school (c) kit

4. The dog has a ____________ of puppies.
(a) case (b) set (c) litter

5. There was a large ____________ of people at the match.
(a) flock (b) litter (c) crowd

6. Mike has a new ____________ of clothes.
(a) clump (b) hive (c) suit

7. Sally ate the whole ____________ of grapes.
(a) tribe (b) bunch (c) flock

8. Dad bought a new ____________ of golf clubs.
(a) book (b) herd (c) set

9. I bought a ____________ of cards.
(a) pack (b) case (c) carton

10. There is a ____________ of garbage at the back of the house.
(a) pile (b) swarm (c) packet

11. Mum brought home a whole ____________ of apples.
(a) crew (b) case (c) nest

12. The ____________ of footballers is on the ground.
(a) team (b) brood (c) hive

UNIT 3 THE FAMILY OF NAMING WORDS YEAR 5

PROPER NOUNS

Proper nouns are words we use to name particular people, places or things. For example, Paul, Mary, England, Thursday. They begin with a capital letter.

Example

Which word is a proper noun?
paper april flower
Answer = ***April*** *(it is a month of the year).*

Write the word in each group that is a proper noun.
Don't forget it should begin with a capital letter.

1. (a) pen (b) book (c) sally

____

2. (a) monday (b) orange (c) cold

____

3. (a) water (b) fish (c) september

____

4. (a) table (b) peter (c) cow

____

5. (a) vietnam (b) man (c) grass

____

6. (a) mrs jones (b) table (c) dog

____

7. (a) july (b) leaf (c) bike

____

8. (a) window (b) melbourne (c) road

____

9. (a) easter (b) flower (c) cat

____

10. (a) thursday (b) fence (c) television

____

11. (a) tree (b) christmas (c) river

____

12. (a) darwin (b) cup (c) spoon

____

UNIT 4 THE FAMILY OF NAMING WORDS PLURAL NOUNS YEAR 5

Plural means *more than one*. Most words add *-s* to form their plural. For example, *dog — dogs, road — roads.*

Words ending in **-*s*, -*ss*, -*ch***, or **-*x*** add **-*es*** to form their plural. For example, ***one glass — two glasses***.

Make the word in brackets mean more than one.
There are two ________ in the paddock. (cow)
*Answer = There are two **cows** in the paddock.*

Now write the correct plural for each of these.

1. This house has six ________ (room).
2. Lots of ________ bring children to our school. (bus)
3. Katy ate two ________ for lunch. (peach)
4. There are three ________ on the shelf. (brush)
5. We saw three ________ in the forest. (fox)
6. I put all the ________ on the table. (box)
7. There are lots of ________ in the garden. (bush)
8. Our school has many ________. (class)
9. There are three ________ in the room. (table)
10. All the ________ were put into the refrigerator. (lunch)
11. There are seven ________ in this street. (church)
12. The doctor used lots of ________ to heal the man's cut. (stitch)

UNIT 5 THE FAMILY OF NAMING WORDS YEAR 5
PLURAL NOUNS

Plural means *more than one*. For example, *one duck — five ducks*.

Nouns that end in ***-y*** with a vowel before the ***-y*** make their plural by adding **-s**.
For example, ***one boy — three boys***.

Nouns that end in ***-y*** and have a consonant before the ***-y*** make their plural by changing ***-y*** to ***-i*** and adding **-es**. For example, ***one fairy — two fairies***.

Write the correct plural in the space.

1. I saw two ________________ at the hospital.
(a) babys (b) babies

2. Susan has lots of ________________.
(a) toys (b) toies

3. I have lost the set of ________________.
(a) keys (b) keies

4. The dog has six ________________.
(a) puppies (b) puppys

5. There are seven ________________ in the tree.
(a) monkeys (b) monkies

6. I went to three ________________ last week.
(a) partys (b) parties

7. We should take good care of our ________________.
(a) bodies (b) bodys

8. We've had lots of ________________ this year.
(a) holidaies (b) holidays

9. I've read many ________________ about dinosaurs.
(a) storys (b) stories

10. This supermarket has two hundred ________________.
(a) trolleys (b) trollies

11. You must not eat too many ________________.
(a) lollys (b) lollies

12. On the farm there are lots of ________________.
(a) turkies (b) turkeys

UNIT 6 THE FAMILY OF NAMING WORDS YEAR 5
PLURAL NOUNS

Plural means *more than one*. Some nouns that end in *-f* or *-fe* make their plurals by changing the *-f* to *-v* and adding *-es*. For example, *loaf — loaves wife wives*.

However there are some exceptions. For example, ***chief – chiefs, roof — roofs***.

Example

Choose the correct plural of the word.
This man has had three ________.
(a) wifes (b) wives
*Answer = (b). This man has had three **wives**.*

Now do these.

1. The baker baked ten ____________ of bread.
(a) loafs (b) loaves

2. The tree has lost all of its ____________.
(a) leaves (b) leafs

3. All the ____________ of the buses are made of metal.
(a) roofs (b) rooves

4. The blacksmith trimmed the horses' ____________.
(a) hoofs (b) hooves

5. The cow had twin ____________.
(a) calfs (b) calves

6. The ____________ were arrested by the police.
(a) thiefs (b) thieves

7. It took her three ____________ to blow out the candles.
(a) puffs (b) puves

8. The five savage ____________ chased the sheep.
(a) wolfs (b) wolves

9. I sharpened the two ____________.
(a) knifes (b) knives

10. I took three ____________ to school with me.
(a) handkerchiefs (b) handkerchieves

11. We read about the ____________ of all the pioneers.
(a) lifes (b) lives

12. Margaret has two ____________ in her favourite team's colours.
(a) scarfs (b) scarves

UNIT 7 THE FAMILY OF NAMING WORDS YEAR 5
PLURAL NOUNS

Some nouns make their plurals by changing a vowel, for example, *one foot — two feet.* Or they add *-en,* for example, *one child — two children.*

Nouns that end in **-o** make their plural in one of two ways.

(a) Some simply add **-s**, for example ***one kangaroo — two kangaroos, one piano — two pianos***.

(b) Some add **-es**, for example ***one tomato — two tomatoes***.

Make the word in brackets mean more than one. Write your answer in the space.

1. The dentist pulled out three of the man's ____________. (tooth)

2. There were three ____________ in the room. (man)

3. I picked six bags of ____________. (potato)

4. I cut up three ____________ for the salad. (tomato)

5. There are over one hundred ____________ in New Zealand. (volcano)

6. I took lots of ____________ on my holiday. (photo)

7. There are lots of ____________ on the farm. (goose)

8. There are twenty ____________ in our grade. (child)

9. My mother said her ____________ were sore. (foot)

10. We have two ____________ in our house. (piano)

11. We saw five ____________ at the zoo. (kangaroo)

12. We caught six ____________ in the trap. (mouse)

UNIT 8 THE FAMILY OF DESCRIBING WORDS ADJECTIVES YEAR 5

Adjectives are words that tell us more about nouns. They can tell what *kind,* what *colour* or *how many.*

For example, They own a **big** house. I have a **red** bike. There are **three** cats.

Example

Choose the best adjective to fill the space.
Bread can be ___________.
(a) pretty (b) stale (c) fast
Answer = ***stale****.*

Now do these.

1. That is a very ___________ knife.
(sharp, green, sick)

2. This ___________ lemon is the ripest.
(fat, quick, yellow)

3. That ___________ music sounds great.
(spicy, loud, baby's)

4. The ___________ smell of the pizza made our mouths water.
(horrible, cheesy, funny)

5. My friend's ___________ bike shines in the sun.
(stolen, sister, new)

6. This ___________ pillow feels as soft as a marshmallow.
(lead, dirty, new)

7. There are ________ days in a week.
(school, seven, easy)

8. The elephant had long ___________ tusks.
(green, pointy, new)

9. The ___________ zebra ran from the lions.
(startled, herd, drinking)

10. The ___________ sun looked like a ball of fire.
(setting, full, brown)

11. He broke his arm when he fell off the ___________ horse.
(galloping, baby, eating)

12. The ___________ baby was crying for milk.
(happy, hungry, girl)

COMPARING ADJECTIVES

Most adjectives add *-er* when comparing two people or things and *-est* when comparing more than two.

For example, *My candle is **brighter** than yours. His candle is the **brightest** of all.*

If the adjective ends in **-e**, this letter is dropped when adding ***-er*** or ***-est***.
For example, *She is the **bravest** person I have ever seen. (brave)*

For adjectives that end in ***-y***, change the ***-y*** to ***-i*** before adding ***-er*** or ***-est***.
For example, *This is the **noisiest** party I have ever been to. (noisy)*

Add the correct form of the adjective in brackets in the space.
Of the six children, Sam is the ____________ (tall).
*Answer = **tallest**.*

Now do these.

1. Of the six kittens, this one is the ____________. (small)
2. Ian is a much ____________ person than David. (wise)
3. This is the ____________ crowd I have ever seen. (large)
4. This dog is much ____________ than that one. (big)
5. I have been ____________ than you lately. (busy)
6. This laneway is much ____________ than that one. (narrow)
7. This torch is the ____________ of all. (bright)
8. This is the ____________ day we have had all year. (hot)
9. Today is ____________ than it was yesterday. (cold)
10. Old Mr Jones is the ____________ person in our street. (healthy)
11. This rock is a lot ____________ than the one you have. (heavy)
12. I feel this is the ____________ spot in the whole world. (safe)

UNIT 10 THE FAMILY OF DOING WORDS — VERBS YEAR 5

Verbs are the most important words in sentences. Every sentence must have at least one verb. Most verbs describe an *action*.

For example, *I* ***am*** *Vietnamese.* *The match* ***has*** *started.* *The dog* ***barked****.*

Example

Choose the best verb to fill the space.
The savage dog ____________ at the burglar.
(a) giggled (b) barked (c) peeled
Answer = The savage dog ***barked*** *at the burglar.*

Now do these.

1. The frogs ____________ all last night.
(a) neighed (b) laughed (c) croaked

2. Amy likes to ____________ sandcastles.
(a) build (b) run (c) cry

3. My horse ____________ down the road.
(a) talks (b) trots (c) bends

4. I ____________ quietly to him.
(a) yelled (b) whispered (c) nailed

5. The lady ____________ the trees in winter.
(a) pruned (b) swallowed (c) hatched

6. John ____________ the dirty clothes.
(a) played (b) beat (c) washed

7. Tim likes to ____________ lemonade.
(a) eat (b) drink (c) ride

8. When it is hot, Grandad likes to ____________ in the pool.
(a) cry (b) swim (c) cook

9. We are ____________ ditches around the tent.
(a) digging (b) eating (c) chopping

10. The kangaroos ____________ over the fence.
(a) hopped (b) swam (c) licked

11. After the long walk they ____________.
(a) rested (b) charged (c) snapped

12. Mia ____________ her hair before going to school.
(a) smoked (b) snored (c) brushed

VERBS — PAST TENSE

A verb in the past tense tells us about something that happened in the past.
For example, I ***played*** yesterday.

(a) Most verbs make their past tense by adding ***-ed***. For example, ***scream — screamed***.
(b) If the verb ends in **-e** then the **-e** is dropped when adding ***-ed***.
For example, ***decide — decided***.
(c) Many verbs form their past tense by doubling the last letter.
For example, ***beg — begged***.
(d) If the present tense ends in ***-y*** this letter is changed to ***-i*** before adding ***-ed***. For example, ***hurry — hurried***.
(e) Instead of adding ***-ed***, some verbs change one or more letters.
For example, ***swim — swam***.

Write the past tense of the verb in brackets in the space.

1. Yesterday our team ___________ the team from the other school. (defeat)

2. This morning we ________ soccer on the oval. (play)

3. Last night I ________ some mushrooms for tea. (cook)

4. We ________ when we met our friends yesterday. (smile)

5. Last night my brother __________ all night. (snore)

6. Last week we ___________ not to go away these holidays. (decide)

7. Last night the car ___________ across the icy road. (skid)

8. This morning I ___________ a glass on to the floor. (drop)

9. The thieves ________ the store last night. (rob)

10. The dog ________ the bone in the garden. (bury)

11. This morning we ________ hard for the spelling test. (study)

12. We ________ a story about snakes this morning. (write)

13. The girl did not reply when I ________ to her. (speak)

14. Effy ________ a picture on the paper. (draw)

UNIT 12 VERBS — AGREEMENT OF SUBJECT AND VERB YEAR 5

The *subject* of a verb must *always agree* with its *verb* in number. If the subject is *singular* then the verb must be *singular*. Similarly, a *plural* subject takes a *plural* verb.

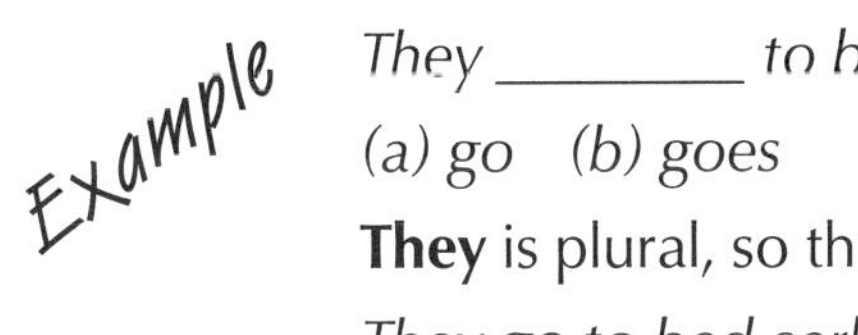

They ________ to bed early.
(a) go (b) goes
They is plural, so the answer is
They ***go*** *to bed early.*

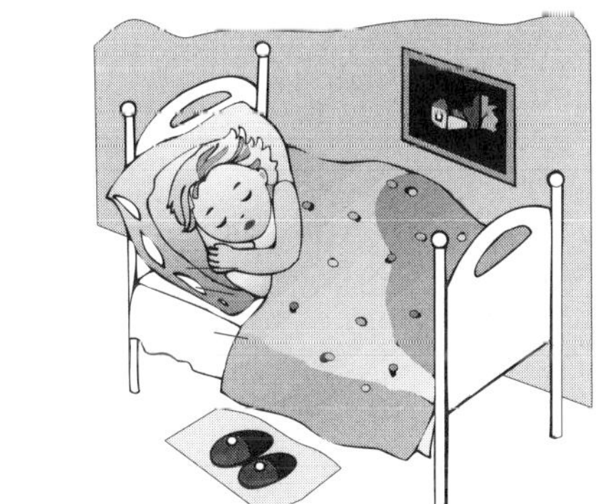

Choose the correct verb to fill each space.

1. Katy ________ her work well.
(a) do (b) does

2. All dogs ________ bones.
(a) like (b) likes

3. The children ________ to school early every day.
(a) come (b) comes

4. Linda always ________ her sneakers to school.
(a) wear (b) wears

5. Our teacher often ________ to my home to see my mother.
(a) come (b) comes

6. The boys ________ pizza for lunch.
(a) eats (b) eat

7. Shane ________ he will be chosen for the team.
(a) hope (b) hopes

8. The savage dog ________ at any stranger.
(a) bark (b) barks

9. My parents ________ to the football every Saturday.
(a) go (b) goes

10. The boys ________ the rooms each day.
(a) clean (b) cleans

11. The teachers take it in turns to ________ us a story every Friday.
(a) read (b) reads

12. Greg ________ a cornet in the school band.
(a) play (b) plays

UNIT 13 VERBS — AGREEMENT OF SUBJECT AND VERB YEAR 5

The subject of a sentence must always agree with its verb in number. If the subject is singular, the verb must be singular.

For example, *The **dog is** barking.* *The **stars are** shining.*
*The **frog was** croaking.* *The **cats were** purring.*
*The **boy has** left.* *The **girls have** arrived.*

However:

(a) **Collective nouns** that are considered as a **single unit** take a singular verb.
For example, *The **team** of footballers **is** on the ground.*

(b) Words denoting **sums of money or quantities** such as length, time, weight and so on, are considered as **units** and take a singular verb.
For example, *Ten **years is** a long time.*

(c) Some nouns that end in **-s** look plural but are really singular.
For example, ***Measles is** an infectious disease.*

Choose the correct word in brackets to fill the space.

1. Pete ____________ going swimming in the pool.
(a) is (b) are

2. The girls ____________ going fishing later.
(a) is (b) are

3. Some of the dogs ____________ barking.
(a) is (b) are

4. Tom ____________ playing in the yard.
(a) was (b) were

5. The girls ____________ swimming in the pool.
(a) was (b) were

6. The flock of birds ____________ in the tree.
(a) was (b) were

7. The boys ____________ left their socks in the gymnasium.
(a) has (b) have

8. The snake ____________ crawled under the rock.
(a) has (b) have

9. Ten dollars ____________ all I had to spend.
(a) was (b) were

10. The horses ____________ been missing for over a week.
(a) has (b) have

11. Six metres ____________ the length of the fence.
(a) is (b) are

12. Smoking cigarettes ____________ a silly thing to do.
(a) is (b) are

UNIT 14 THE FAMILY OF HELPING WORDS – ADVERBS YEAR 5

Adverbs are words that tell us something about *verbs* and add meaning to them. Adverbs usually tell us *how, when* or *where*.

For example, *Sam walked* ***slowly***. (How he walked)
Jack will leave ***soon***. (When he will leave)
We played ***outside***. (Where we played)

Example

Choose the best adverb to fill the space.
The baby cried ____________.
(a) happily (b) loudly (c) greedily
Answer = The baby cried ***loudly.***

Now do these.

1. The car lights are shining ____________.
(a) quickly (b) brightly (c) sadly

2. Some children write ____________.
(a) neatly (b) sweetly (c) over

3. It is hot ____________ the car.
(a) inside (b) around (c) happily.

4. Everyone was laughing ____________.
(a) sadly (b) happily (c) rapidly

5. She tied the knot ____________.
(a) coolly (b) tightly (c) brightly

6. The moon will shine ____________.
(a) tonight (b) yesterday (c) loudly

7. Margaret yawned ____________.
(a) wearily (b) down (c) busily

8. I ____________ look before crossing a busy road.
(a) never (b) always (c) soon

9. The cat crept ____________ towards the mouse.
(a) hardly (b) silently (c) loudly

10. The frightened horse galloped

____________ across the paddock.
(a) quickly (b) slowly (c) softly

11. Rain comes ____________ from the sky.
(a) up (b) down (c) beside

12. We must leave ____________ or we will get wet.
(a) yesterday (b) soon (c) down

UNIT 15 THE FAMILY OF PEOPLE AND THING WORDS YEAR 5
PRONOUNS

Pronouns are words that we use *instead of nouns*. In fact, a pronoun is a word that could be replaced by a noun.

For example, *John kicked the dog and the dog bit John.*

This is clumsy! We can replace the second **John** with **him** and the second **dog** with **it**.

*John kicked the dog and **it** bit **him**.*

Here are the pronouns we often use.

I	we	me	them	his/her	their
you	you	us	our	its	mine
he/she/it	they	him/her/it	my	your	yours

Choose the pronouns to go in each space.

1. The tree lost __________ leaves.
(a) its (b) their (c) they

2. Jacob is my friend and I play with __________ at school.
(a) her (b) him (c) she

3. Give __________ back my pen please.
(a) you (b) me (c) she

4. I saw three birds and __________ looked like magpies.
(a) it (b) they (c) their

5. Mary rode down the street and __________ saw two cars crash.
(a) they (b) she (c) their

6. The birds were hungry so we fed __________.
(a) those (b) them (c) their

7. Max and __________ went camping last weekend.
(a) its (b) his (c) I

8. This pen belongs to me. This pen is __________.
(a) ours (b) mine (c) hers

9. The girls left __________ bicycles in the backyard.
(a) his (b) hers (c) their

10. Joshua built the house all by __________.
(a) himself (b) me (c) yours

11. These books belong to you. They are __________.
(a) yours (b) his (c) herself

12. Mr Smith gave Ellen and __________ some eggs.
(a) me (b) it (c) mine

THE FAMILY OF JOINING WORDS CONJUNCTIONS

A conjunction is a word which joins together two single words or two groups of words.

For example, *fish **and** chips*
*He did not come **because** he was ill.*

Here are some conjunctions we often use:

if	as	and	but	yet	that	when	since
until	though	unless	because	whether	although	while	or

Example

Choose the conjunction that best completes the sentence.
Mother paid the butcher ________ put the meat in her basket.
(a) yet (b) and (c) while
*Answer = Mother paid the butcher **and** put the meat in her basket.*

Now do these.

1. The wind was cold, ____________ it was the middle of winter.
(a) so (b) because (c) whether

2. Bill did not come ______________ he promised he would.
(a) until (b) although (c) into

3. Mel cooked the eggs _________ I buttered the toast.
(a) until (b) and (c) since

4. I have not seen Joseph _________ last year.
(a) although (b) since (c) because

5. I will not share the lollies _________ you help me.
(a) yet (b) that (c) unless

6. Let us sit here ________ the rain stops falling.
(a) and (b) until (c) though

7. We met a Frenchman ______________ name was Pierre.
(a) who (b) whose (c) which

8. ______________ he did not study, Rick failed the test.
(a) But (b) Because (c) Until

9. ______________ they searched all night, the police did not find the lost girl.
(a) Although (b) Until (c) And

10. ______________ the boy was bitten by a snake, the doctor was called.
(a) Although (b) After (c) Until

11. The rivers will flood ______________ the heavy rain continues.
(a) although (b) if (c) so

12. We will not win ______________ our best player can be in the team.
(a) unless (b) and (c) before

UNIT 17 THE FAMILY OF PLACE WORDS — PREPOSITIONS YEAR 5

A *preposition* shows the relationship between a noun, or pronoun, and another word, in a sentence.

For example, *The cat is **on** the table.* *The cat is hiding **under** the table.*

Remember:
(a) Something is shared **between** two people but **among** three or more.
(b) One thing or person is different **from** another. (**Never** say different **to** or different **than**.)
(c) **In** shows position in **one** place while **into** shows movement from one place to another.

For example, *The eggs are **in** the nest. He dived from the tree **into** the water.*

Example

Choose the best preposition to fill the space.
The glass is full ___________ milk.
(a) off (b) of (c) under
*Answer = The glass is full **of** milk.*

Now do these.

1. Some people say milk is good ___________ us.
(a) above (b) on (c) for

2. Be careful you don't knock the cup ___________ the table.
(a) off (b) beside (c) above

3. We took cover in the barn ___________ the storm.
(a) behind (b) during (c) at

4. The snake crawled ___________ the rock.
(a) with (b) after (c) under

5. I shared the lollies ___________ my five friends.
(a) among (b) under (c) between

6. We get our meat ___________ the supermarket.
(a) near (b) off (c) from

7. When it rains I always go ___________ the house.
(a) outside (b) inside (c) above

8. The kangaroo hopped ___________ the fence.
(a) from (b) over (c) with

9. The apricots are ___________ the box.
(a) into (b) in (c) along

10. He fell from the roof ___________ the pool.
(a) in (b) into (c) among

11. The two boys shared the coins ___________ them.
(a) between (b) among (c) over

12. The moon is ___________ the clouds.
(a) above (b) into (c) off

CORRECT USAGE

Sometimes we make errors when we write or speak. We can choose the wrong *tense*, or use *verbs* which don't *agree* with their *subject*, or use a word that *doesn't make sense* in the sentence.

Example

Which word correctly fills the space?
She ___________ her arm.
(a) hurt (b) hurted
The word 'hurt' does not add *-ed* to make the past tense, so the correct answer is: *She* ***hurt*** *her arm.*

Now choose the correct word to fill each space.

1. "We ___________ going to come," said John.
(a) ain't (b) aren't

2. ___________ I have some more cake?
(a) Can (b) May

3. Fran sings ___________.
(a) good (b) well

4. I cannot run ___________ further.
(a) no (b) any

5. She ___________ a bad accident.
(a) had (b) got

6. George gave it back to ___________.
(a) I (b) me

7. Yesterday Nguyen ___________ to me.
(a) speak (b) spoke

8. There ___________ five birds in the cage.
(a) is (b) are

9. Jesse is ___________ than Julie.
(a) older (b) oldest

10. The books ___________ we read were interesting.
(a) what (b) that

11. Susan has ___________ her leg.
(a) broke (b) broken

12. I ___________ him walk into the cafe.
(a) saw (b) seen

A *phrase* is a group of words. Sometimes we use a phrase or several words when one word will do.

Example

Which word best takes the place of the bold words?
*I threw out the **skin of the orange**.*
(a) paper (b) peel (c) sun
*Answer = (b). I threw out the **peel**.*

Circle the word which can replace the phrase, and write the new sentence.

1. The **wood for building** is in the yard.
(a) trees (b) timber (c) animal

____

____

2. Some **frozen water** is in the cup.
(a) ice (b) wood (c) air

____

____

3. The light started to **become less bright.**
(a) jump (b) fade (c) play

____

____

4. I had a **short sleep** after lunch.
(a) nap (b) play (c) cry

____

____

5. This old knife is **helpful to have.**
(a) useful (b) silly (c) cheap

____

____

6. I put the books on the **narrow shelf.**
(a) cupboard (b) table (c) ledge

____

____

7. The bird used a **small branch** for its nest.
(a) leaf (b) twig (c) camel

____

____

8. I began to **wash and iron** my clothes.
(a) dirty (b) crunch (c) launder

____

____

9. The meat was **chopped into small pieces.**
(a) minced (b) sold (c) frozen

____

____

10. This old table is **very hard to lift.**
(a) icy (b) light (c) heavy

____

____

UNIT 20 THE FAMILY OF WORD GROUPS YEAR 5

SENTENCES — SENTENCE STRUCTURE

A sentence is a group of words which expresses a complete thought; in other words, it *makes sense.*

Which of these expresses a complete thought and is therefore a sentence?
(a) when it was six o'clock *(b) The bear chased the deer.*
Answer = (b). ***The bear chased the deer.***
(a) does not make sense by itself as we need to know what happened when it was six o'clock.

Circle the complete sentence in each pair below. Make the second sentence a complete sentence and write it in the space.

1. (a) One evening in July.
(b) We ate pizza for lunch.

2. (a) A kangaroo carries its young in a pouch.
(b) In the centre of Melbourne.

3. (a) Mike was voted captain of our team.
(b) With a lot of sadness.

4. (a) Inside the old building.
(b) Cows can bellow.

5. (a) We grow flowers in a garden.
(b) Beside the old windmill.

6. (a) Kicking the football.
(b) I like to play golf.

7. (a) All of a sudden.
(b) Please come here.

8. (a) Did you see the jet?
(b) On the table.

9. (a) Have you been to Melbourne?
(b) Combed his hair.

10. (a) Bill has a new.
(b) A bee makes honey.

UNIT 21 THE FAMILY OF WORD GROUPS SENTENCES — COMPREHENSION YEAR 5

Read this passage then circle the correct answers.

My father, John Ridd, had been killed by the Doones of Bagworthy while riding home from Porlock market with six other farmers one Saturday evening. These robbers had no grudge against him, for he never flouted them because they robbed other people. The seven were jogging along when suddenly a horseman stopped in the starlight full across them, and though he seemed one man against seven it was really one man against one, for of the six who were with my father, there was not one who did not pull out his money.

1. John Ridd was
(a) a teacher. (b) a farmer.

2. John Ridd was riding home with
(a) six others. (b) ten others.

3. The men were riding
(a) bikes. (b) horses.

4. The men had been at
(a) a market. (b) a picnic.

5. The family name of the person telling the story is
(a) Doone. (b) Ridd.

6. The man was killed
(a) in the morning.
(b) in the evening.

7. The day before John Ridd was killed was
(a) Sunday. (b) Friday.

8. The Doones were
(a) robbers. (b) farmers.

9. The Doones lived at
(a) Bagworthy. (b) Porlock.

10. Counting the farmers and the robber, altogether there were
(a) seven people. (b) eight people.

11. The robber wanted their
(a) horses. (b) money.

12. When the robbers appeared the farmers' horses were
(a) galloping quickly.
(b) jogging along.

UNIT 22 THE FAMILY OF WORD GROUPS — SENTENCES YEAR 5
DRAWING CONCLUSIONS FROM GIVEN INFORMATION

Look at the people's occupations in the box. Write them beside the sentence you think each person may have said.

waiter	policeman	farmer	teacher
doctor	veterinarian	pilot	angler
cashier	gardener	photographer	dentist

1. After we finish our spelling we'll go out for a game.

 ____

2. I will have to put a filling in this back molar.

 ____

3. This is the best wheat crop I've had for years.

 ____

4. How would you like your steak: medium or rare?

 ____

5. We should be landing at the Melbourne Airport in 10 minutes.

 ____

6. I want you to look directly at the camera and say "cheese".

 ____

7. Your blood pressure is a little high today.

 ____

8. May I see your driver's licence please?

 ____

9. Hold its collar tight and I'll give your dog this needle.

 ____

10. I think I've hooked a large cod.

 ____

11. These groceries add up to seventy two dollars, sir.

 ____

12. My carrots should be ready for eating in a week.

 ____

UNIT 23 THE FAMILY OF WORD GROUPS — SENTENCES YEAR 5
SELECTING IMPORTANT INFORMATION

It is important, when reading for information, to be able to decide which information is valuable and which is of no real importance.

Example

Which of these sentences give us the most information about bees?
(a) Bees like to buzz about.
(b) Bees are insects that pollinate flowers.
Answer = (b). Bees are insects that pollinate flowers.

Circle the sentence in each pair that gives us the most information.

1. (a) The flowers of a plant are necessary for the making of seeds.
(b) Some flowers are red.

2. (a) Captain James Cook did not like school.
(b) Captain James Cook discovered the east coast of Australia.

3. (a) All birds have feathers and lay eggs.
(b) Some parrots can learn to talk.

4. (a) Only some children like oranges.
(b) Oranges are citrus fruits and contain lots of Vitamin C.

5. (a) Sharks are scary animals that might eat you.
(b) Of the many types of sharks, only a few are dangerous to humans.

6. (a) The goanna is a large native lizard.
(b) Some lizards lay eggs.

7. (a) Some ants like to eat sugar.
(b) Termites are not really "white ants" but are actually small beetles.

8. (a) At school we learn to read and write.
(b) I like school holidays.

9. (a) We went to Melbourne once.
(b) Melbourne is the largest city in Victoria.

10. (a) Horses have four legs.
(b) Horses helped early pioneers to develop farmlands.

11. Describe yourself in two sentences. Which information do you think is the most important to include?

____

____

12. Now describe your best friend in two sentences.

____

____

UNIT 24 PUNCTUATION CAPITAL LETTERS AND FULL STOPS YEAR 5

A *statement* always begins with a capital letter and ends with a full stop.

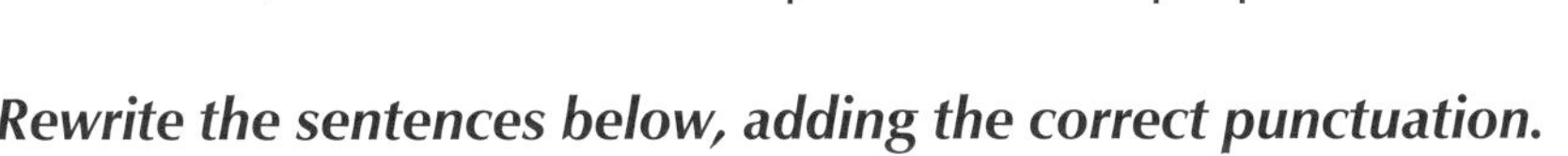

Example *it is nearly seven o'clock* should be written
It is nearly seven o'clock.

Remember, we must also use capital letters for proper nouns. (See Unit 3.)

Rewrite the sentences below, adding the correct punctuation.

1. my dog's name is spot

____

2. i saw bill on the swing

____

3. freya is the tallest girl in our year

____

4. tom and susan both come from brisbane

____

____

5. when peter was in perth he met john in wattle street

____

____

6. tom told us that con was ten years old last monday

____

____

7. vietnam and china are both countries in asia

____

8. our teacher mrs smith was away last friday

____

9. mercury and venus are two planets

____

10. when it is the first saturday in april it will be sam's birthday

____

11. the murray river forms a border between victoria and new south wales

____

____

12. nick and susan are going to sydney next christmas

____

____

Statements always begin with capital letters and end with full stops. For example, *I read a book about snakes.*

In each question there are two sentences. Add the capital letters and full stops where they are needed.

our neighbours have bought a new car it is a blue mazda
Our neighbours have bought a new car. It is a blue Mazda.

Now do these.

1. john went to the zoo he saw lots of wild animals

2. tokyo is a large city it is the capital of japan

3. bees are very useful to us they pollinate flowers to make honey

4. a dromedary is a type of camel it has only one hump

5. i have lost my pen please help me find it

6. veronica is ten years old tomorrow she is having a party next saturday

7. eskimos live in cold lands they build homes from blocks of ice

8. these flowers look beautiful they are a type of daisy

9. melbourne is a large city it is twenty kilometres from here

10. The child was very ill he ate some poisonous toadstools

11. jane has a new puppy its name is spot

12. next week the holidays begin i am going to brisbane

A *statement* begins with a capital letter and ends with a full stop.

For example, *It is hot today.*

A *question* begins with a capital letter and ends with a question mark.

For example, *Why is the baby crying?*

Rewrite each sentence, adding the missing capital letters, full stops and question marks.

1. (a) where is sam
(b) he is in the gymnasium

(a) ______________________________

(b) ______________________________

2. (a) what colour is a penguin
(b) it is black and white

(a) ______________________________

(b) ______________________________

3. (a) it is nearly four o'clock
(b) what is the time

(a) ______________________________

(b) ______________________________

4. (a) a jockey rides horses in races
(b) what does a jockey do

(a) ______________________________

(b) ______________________________

5. (a) what animal is called the ship of the desert
(b) it is a camel

(a) ______________________________

(b) ______________________________

6. (a) it has eight legs
(b) how many legs does a spider have?

(a) ______________________________

(b) ______________________________

7. (a) why do birds fly north in winter
(b) it is too far to walk

(a) ______________________________

(b) ______________________________

8. (a) it is a type of flower
(b) what is a crocus

(a) ______________________________

(b) ______________________________

9. (a) when is mike's birthday
(b) his birthday was last saturday

(a) ______________________________

(b) ______________________________

10. (a) it is on the 25th of december
(b) when is christmas day

(a) ______________________________

(b) ______________________________

UNIT 27 PUNCTUATION — STATEMENTS AND QUESTIONS YEAR 5

A *statement* begins with a capital letter and ends with a full stop.
For example, ***I*** *brushed my hair***.**

A **question** begins with a capital letter and ends with a question mark.
For example, ***D****id you brush your hair***?**

i met the new boy have you met him
I *met the new boy***. H***ave you met him***?**

Rewrite the sentences with correct punctuation.

1. i don't like pies do you like them

2. my birthday is tomorrow when is yours

3. jade has a new bicycle have you seen it

4. where did you put my pen i want it back

5. my parents come from vietnam where do yours come from

6. is bill at school today i haven't seen him at all

7. what colour is a zebra it is black and white

8. who won the match i didn't hear the result

9. what colour is your bicycle mine is a red colour

10. i have to dry the dishes will you help me

11. have you read the story about robin hood it is very exciting

12. mr smith cuts my hair does he cut your hair too

PUNCTUATION — THE COMMA

(a) One way we use a comma is to **separate words** in a list.
For example, *We saw cows donkeys horses sheep and cattle on the farm.*
We saw cows, donkeys, horses, sheep and cattle on the farm.

(b) Another way is to **separate groups** of words.
For example, *We looked under the table near the chair and on top of the heater but couldn't find it.*
We looked under the table, near the chair, and on top of the heater, but couldn't find it.

(c) Commas also separate words that **stand for the same thing**.
For example, *My friend Debbie is coming.*
My friend, Debbie, is coming.

Rewrite each sentence using the correct punctuation.

1. Four planets are Venus Mars Earth and Jupiter.

____

____

2. My favourite fruits are bananas oranges apples grapes and apricots.

____

____

3. The four seasons are summer autumn winter and spring.

____

____

4. Eels sharks cod and herring are all types of fish.

____

____

5. Football soccer tennis netball softball and cricket are all sports.

____

____

6. The nearest planet to the sun Mercury is extremely hot.

____

____

7. My brother Sam likes to play football.

____

____

8. Lisa's best friend Joanne is coming to the party.

____

____

9. The frightened horse galloped out of its stable along the road across the backyard and then was caught by Mr Smith.

____

____

10. Our teacher Mrs Jones looked in her purse under her table on top of the desk and inside the drawer but couldn't find her car keys.

____

____

PUNCTUATION — CONTRACTIONS

A contraction is a *shortened form* of two or more words.

For example, ***didn't*** *is a contraction of* ***did not****.*

He'd *been playing cricket.*
Answer = ***He had****.*

Write the two words that make up each contraction.

1. I **don't** like eating eggs.

   ____

2. She **can't** help you now.

   ____

3. I **won't** help you unless you try harder.

   ____

4. **We're** leaving soon.

   ____

5. **It's** very cold today.

   ____

6. Bill **isn't** at school today.

   ____

7. **We've** looked everywhere but can't find it.

   ____

8. She said **they'd** be here soon.

   ____

9. If you want me to, **I'll** help you lift it.

   ____

10. Sam **couldn't** find his lost puppy.

    ____

11. "**Let's** get some fairy floss," said Sally.

    ____

12. **How's** your uncle going?

    ____

13. Sam **doesn't** like his new teacher.

    ____

14. **They're** not going to the disco after all.

    ____

UNIT 30 PUNCTUATION — DIRECT SPEECH YEAR 5

When we write what a person has said, we always enclose it in *inverted commas* (“ ”). Inverted commas are also called *quotation marks* or *speech marks*.

Example

John said, I can’t find my pen.
The actual words spoken by John were **I can’t find my pen**, so we enclose these words in inverted commas.
John said, “I can’t find my pen.”

Notice that the full stop goes **inside** the inverted commas. Other punctuation, such as **question marks** and **exclamation marks** also go inside the **inverted commas**.

Also notice that we add a comma before the inverted commas, to separate what is **being said** from the person who is **saying it**. For example, *John said**,** “I can’t find my pen.”*

If the spoken words come **before** the speaker’s name, we still use a comma to separate them, but we put the comma **inside** the inverted commas, For example, *“I can’t find my pen,” John said.*

Add inverted commas around the words actually said in each sentence. Also, add commas and full stops where they are needed.

1. Mike said I am ready to go now

   ____

   ____

2. Samantha yelled Hey wait for me

   ____

   ____

3. Chan whispered Don’t forget to bring your bathers

   ____

   ____

4. There are six boys in the room said John

   ____

   ____

5. My parents are going to Melbourne next week said Joanne

   ____

   ____

6. Where are my socks asked Susan

   ____

   ____

7. Tommy cried I don’t want to eat any more porridge

   ____

   ____

8. When does the train arrive asked the lady

   ____

   ____

9. Why won’t you let me have some lollies complained Paul

   ____

   ____

10. I am not feeling very well said Joseph

   ____

   ____

[ ] denotes the unit to refer to.

1. Which word is the name of something?
(a) running (b) table (c) pretty **[1]**

2. Which word best fills the space?
I heard a __________ of geese fly over.
(a) mob (b) bunch (c) flock **[2]**

3. Circle the words that are proper nouns (those words that should begin with a capital letter).
Last july I went swimming in the river. **[3]**

4. Make each word mean more than one.

one tree	two ________	**[4]**
one bunch	three ________	**[4]**
one city	two________	**[5]**
a knife	two________	**[6]**
one volcano	six ________	**[7]**

5. In this sentence circle the word that describes the dog.
Yesterday the large dog barked loudly at the intruder. **[8]**

6. Circle the correct word that would fill the space.
This is the ________ building in the city.
(tall taller tallest) **[9]**

7. Circle the correct word.
(a) Tom likes to ________ hot tea.
(play drink hope) **[10]**
(b) Mike _______ a picture on paper.
(drew draw drawed) **[11]**
(c) Tom ________ his work well.
(do does) **[12]**
(d) The girls ______ here now.
(is are) **[13]**

8. Circle the word that describes how Sally yawned.
Sally yawned wearily before going to bed. **[14]**

9. Circle the word that would take the place of the bold word.
Yesterday Bill went to their house and **Bill** knocked on their door.
(she they he) **[15]**

10. Circle the word which would best join these two sentences.
Mike dug the soil. I planted the seeds.
(whose unless and) **[16]**

11. Which word best fills the space?
He dived from the tree ________ the river.
(a) into (b) in (c) off **[17]**

12. Which word best fills the space?
John can run __________.
(fast quick) **[18]**

13. Which word means the same as the bold words?
The man **without hair** is in the foyer.
(a) silly (b) old (c) bald **[19]**

14. Which of these is a complete sentence?
(a) After ten o'clock. (b) It is nearly dark. **[20]**

15. Read the sentence, then answer the question.
Jeffrey's mother, Jan Swift, is a famous author.
What is Jeffrey's last name? __________ **[21]**

16. Circle the person who is most likely to say, "When I finish this essay we can go."
(a) a grandmother (b) a salesperson
(c) a student **[22]**

17. Tick the sentence which gives the most information about trees:
(a) Some trees are very tall.
(b) Trees can be deciduous or evergreen. **[23]**

18. Punctuate the following correctly:
sally is leaving for melbourne next april billy will go with her **[24, 25]**

19. Punctuate the following correctly:
is joe coming yes he will be here soon **[26, 27]**

20. Add the missing commas.
Sue my best friend likes to play hockey netball and cricket. **[28]**

21. Write the two words that make up this contraction.
I'll _________ __________ **[29]**

22. Add inverted commas around what is actually being said. (You may also need to add a comma.)
I am ready to leave now yelled Mike. **[30]**

UNIT 1 Nouns

1. c 2. a 3. c 4. c 5. b 6. a
7. a 8. c 9. Saturday morning, breakfast, Tim, Ian, Katy, hats, trainers, creek, buckets, oranges, net, school, competition, tadpoles, frogs, hill, something, creek, nets, buckets, kids, school, tadpoles, Farmer's Creek.

UNIT 2 Collective Nouns

1. b 2. a 3. a 4. c 5. c 6. c
7. b 8. c 9. a 10. a 11. b 12. a

UNIT 3 Proper Nouns

1. Sally 2. Monday 3. September
4. Peter 5. Vietnam 6. Mrs Jones
7. July 8. Melbourne 9. Easter
10. Thursday 11. Christmas 12. Darwin

UNIT 4 Plural Nouns

1. rooms 2. buses 3. peaches 4. brushes
5. foxes 6. boxes 7. bushes 8. classes
9. tables 10. lunches 11. churches 12. stitches

UNIT 5 Plural Nouns

1. b 2. a 3. a 4. a 5. a 6. b
7. a 8. b 9. b 10. a 11. b 12. b

UNIT 6 Plural Nouns

1. b 2. a 3. a 4. a 5. b 6. b
7. a 8. b 9. b 10. a 11. b 12. b

UNIT 7 Plural Nouns

1. teeth 2. men 3. potatoes 4. tomatoes
5. volcanoes 6. photos 7. geese 8. children
9. feet 10. pianos 11. kangaroos 12. mice

UNIT 8 Adjectives

1. sharp 2. yellow 3. loud 4. cheesy
5. new 6. new 7. seven 8. pointy
9. startled 10. setting 11. galloping 12. hungry

UNIT 9 Comparing Adjectives

1. smallest 2. wiser 3. largest
4. bigger 5. busier 6. narrower
7. brightest 8. hottest 9. colder
10. healthiest 11. heavier 12. safest

UNIT 10 Verbs

1. c 2. a 3. b 4. b 5. a 6. c
7. b 8. b 9. a 10. a 11. a 12. c

UNIT 11 Verbs — Past Tense

1. defeated 2. played 3. cooked 4. smiled
5. snored 6. decided 7. skidded 8. dropped
9. robbed 10. buried 11. studied 12. wrote
13. spoke 14. drew

UNIT 12 Agreement of Subject and Verb

1. b 2. a 3. a 4. b 5. b 6. b
7. b 8. b 9. a 10. a 11. a 12. b

UNIT 13 Agreement of Subject and Verb

1. is 2. are 3. are 4. was
5. were 6. was 7. have 8. has
9. was 10. have 11. is 12. is

UNIT 14 Adverbs

1. b 2. a 3. a 4. b 5. b 6. a
7. a 8. b 9. b 10. a 11. b 12. b

UNIT 15 Pronouns

1. a 2. b 3. b 4. b 5. b 6. b
7. c 8. b 9. c 10. a 11. a 12. a

UNIT 16 Conjunctions

1. b 2. b 3. b 4. b 5. c 6. b
7. b 8. b 9. a 10. b 11. b 12. a

UNIT 17 Prepositions

1. c 2. a 3. b 4. c 5. a 6. c
7. b 8. b 9. b 10. b 11. a 12. a

UNIT 18 Correct Usage

1. b 2. b 3. b 4. b 5. a 6. b
7. b 8. b 9. a 10. b 11. b 12. a

UNIT 19 Phrases

1. The **timber** is in the yard. 2. Some **ice** is in the cup.
3. The light started to **fade**. 4. I had a **nap** after lunch.
5. This old knife is **useful**. 6. I put the books on the **ledge**.
7. The bird used a **twig** for its nest.
8. I began to **launder** my clothes. 9. The meat was **minced**. 10. This old table is **heavy**.

UNIT 20 Sentence Structure

1. b 2. a 3. a 4. b 5. a 6. b
7. b 8. a 9. a 10. b
Complete sentences will vary but check for sense, full stops and capital letters.

UNIT 21 Comprehension

1. b 2. a 3. b 4. a 5. b 6. b
7. b 8. a 9. a 10. b 11. b 12. b

UNIT 22 Drawing Conclusions

1. teacher 2. dentist 3. farmer 4. waiter
5. pilot 6. photographer 7. doctor 8. policeman
9. veterinarian 10. angler 11. cashier 12. gardener

UNIT 23 Selecting Important Information

1. a 2. b 3. a 4. b 5. b 6. a
7. b 8. a 9. b 10. b
11. and 12. Answers will vary.

UNIT 24 Capital Letters & Full Stops

1. My dog's name is Spot.
2. I saw Bill on the swing.
3. Freya is the tallest girl in our year.
4. Tom and Susan both come from Brisbane.
5. When Peter was in Perth he met John in Wattle Street.

6. Tom told us that Con was ten years old last Monday.
7. Vietnam and China are both countries in Asia.
8. Our teacher, Mrs Smith, was away last Friday.
9. Mercury and Venus are two planets.
10. When it is the first Saturday in April it will be Sam's birthday.
11. The Murray River forms a border between Victoria and New South Wales.
12. Nick and Susan are going to Sydney next Christmas.

UNIT 25 Statements

1. John went to the zoo. He saw lots of wild animals.
2. Tokyo is a large city. It is the capital of Japan.
3. Bees are very useful to us. They pollinate flowers to make honey.
4. A dromedary is a type of camel. It has only one hump.
5. I have lost my pen. Please help me find it.
6. Veronica is ten years old tomorrow. She is having a party next Saturday.
7. Eskimos live in cold lands. They build homes from blocks of ice.
8. These flowers look beautiful. They are a type of daisy.
9. Melbourne is a large city. It is twenty kilometres from here.
10. The child is very ill. He ate some poisonous toadstools.
11. Jane has a new puppy. Its name is Spot.
12. Next week the holidays begin. I am going to Brisbane.

UNIT 26 Statements and Questions

1. (a) Where is Sam? (b) He is in the gymnasium.
2. (a) What colour is a penguin? (b) It is black and white.
3. (a) It is nearly four o'clock. (b) What is the time?
4. (a) A jockey rides horses in races.
(b) What does a jockey do?
5. (a) What animal is called the ship of the desert?
(b) It is a camel.
6. (a) It has eight legs. (b) How many legs does a spider have?
7. (a) Why do birds fly north in winter? (b) It is too far to walk.
8. (a) It is a type of flower. (b) What is a crocus?
9. (a) When is Mike's birthday?
(b) His birthday was last Saturday.
10. (a) It is on the 25th of December.
(b) When is Christmas Day?

UNIT 27 Statements and Questions

1. I don't like pies. Do you like them?
2. My birthday is tomorrow. When is yours?
3. Jack has a new bicycle. Have you seen it?
4. Where did you put my pen? I want it back.
5. My parents come from Vietnam. Where do yours come from?
6. Is Bill at school today? I haven't seen him at all.
7. What colour is a zebra? It is black and white.
8. Who won the match? I didn't hear the result.
9. What colour is your bicycle? Mine is a red colour.
10. I have to dry the dishes. Will you help me?
11. Have you read the story about Robin Hood? It is very exciting.
12. Mr Smith cuts my hair. Does he cut your hair too?

UNIT 28 The Comma

1. Four planets are Venus, Mars, Earth and Jupiter.
2. My favourite fruits are bananas, oranges, apples, grapes and apricots.
3. The four seasons are summer, autumn, winter and spring.
4. Eels, sharks, cod and herring are all types of fish.
5. Football, soccer, tennis, netball, softball and cricket are all sports.
6. The nearest planet to the sun, Mercury, is extremely hot.
7. My brother, Sam, likes to play football.
8. Lisa's best friend, Joanne, is coming to the party.
9. The frightened horse galloped out of its stable, along the road, across the backyard and then was caught by Mr Smith.
10. Our teacher, Mrs Jones, looked in her purse, under her table, on top of the desk and inside the drawer but couldn't find her car keys.

UNIT 29 Contractions

1. do not	2. can not	3. will not
4. We are	5. It is	6. is not
7. We have	8. they would	9. I will
10. could not	11. Let us	12. How is
13. does not	14. They are	

UNIT 30 Direct Speech

1. Mike said, "I am ready to go now."
2. Samantha yelled, "Hey wait for me."
3. Chan whispered, "Don't forget to bring your bathers."
4. "There are six boys in the room," said John.
5. "My parents are going to Melbourne next week," said Joanne.
6. "Where are my socks?" asked Susan.
7. Tommy cried, "I don't want to eat any more porridge."
8. "When does the train arrive?" asked the lady.
9. "Why won't you let me have some lollies?" complained Paul.
10. "I am not feeling well," said Joseph.

MASTERY TEST

1. table 2. flock 3. July
4. trees, bunches, cities, knives, volcanoes
5. large 6. tallest
7. (a) drink (b) drew (c) does (d) are 8. wearily
9. he 10. and 11. into
12. fast 13. The **bald** man is in the foyer.
14. b 15. Swift 16. c
17. b 18. Sally is leaving for Melbourne next April. Billy will go with her.
19. Is Joe coming? Yes, he will be here soon.
20. Sue, my best friend, likes to play hockey, netball and cricket. 21. I will.
22. "I am ready to leave now," yelled Mike.

UNIT 1 **Nouns**
1. a 2. c 3. a 4. c 5. a 6. c
7. b 8. a 9. a 10. a 11. b 12. a

UNIT 2 **Collective Nouns**
1. c 2. b 3. a 4 b 5 c 6. a
7 b 8. b 9. a 10. b 11. a 12. b

UNIT 3 **Proper Nouns**
1. Friday 2. James 3. Perth 4. July
5. Norway 6. Christmas 7. Yarra River
8. Easter 9. Spencer Street 10. Victoria
11. Mrs Smith 12. Mazda 13-17. Answers will vary.

UNIT 4 **Plural Nouns**
1. buses 2. apples 3. dresses 4. churches
5. foxes 6. boxes 7. brushes 8. watches
9. wishes 10. classes 11. crusts 12. gases

UNIT 5 **Plural Nouns**
1. b 2. b 3. b 4. b 5. b 6. b
7. a 8. a 9. b 10. b 11. b 12. b

UNIT 6 **Plural Nouns**
1. volcanoes 2. dingoes 3. kangaroos
4. tomatoes 5. photos 6. mosquitoes
7. pliers 8. sheep 9. jeans
10. geese 11. teeth 12. mice

UNIT 7 **Adjectives**
1. b 2. c 3. a 4. b 5. a 6. a
7. c 8. c 9. a 10. b 11. a 12. c

UNIT 8 **Comparing Adjectives**
1. smallest 2. taller 3. largest
4. wiser 5. luckiest 6. safer
7. hottest 8. fatter 9. most honest
10. more delicious 11. less 12. worst

UNIT 9 **Proper Adjectives**
1. Danish 2. Welsh 3. French 4. Dutch
5. Mexican 6. Swiss 7. Chinese 8. Canadian
9. Turkish 10. Scottish 11. Spanish 12. Swedish

UNIT 10 **Verbs**
1. b 2. a 3. b 4. a 5. c 6. b
7. c 8. a 9. a 10. a 11. a 12. c

UNIT 11 **Verbs — Tense**
1. screamed 2. repeated 3. decided 4. wasted
5. described 6. copied 7. replied 8. buried
9. travelled 10. dripped 11. taught 12. chose

UNIT 12 **Agreement of Subject and Verb**
1. a 2. b 3. b 4. a 5. a 6. a
7. b 8. b 9. a 10. a 11. a 12. a

UNIT 13 **Adverbs**
1. sweetly 2. quickly 3. suddenly
4. proudly 5. angrily 6. easily
7. noisily 8. gently 9. sensibly
10. carefully 11. hopefully 12. accidentally

UNIT 14 **Pronouns**
1. a 2. c 3. b 4. b 5. b 6. a
7. c 8. a 9. b 10. b 11. a 12. b

UNIT 15 **Conjunctions**
1. c 2. a 3. b 4. a 5. a 6. c
7. b 8. b 9. b 10. c 11. b 12. b

UNIT 16 **Prepositions**
1. c 2. b 3. b 4. b 5. b 6. b
7. a 8. b 9. a 10. c 11. b 12. c

UNIT 17 **Correct Usage**
1. b 2. a 3. b 4. a 5. b 6. b
7. a 8. b 9. a 10. b 11. a 12. b

UNIT 18 **Correct Usage**
1. b 2. b 3. b 4. a 5. b 6. b
7. a 8. b 9. b 10. a 11. b 12. b
13. b 14. b

UNIT 19 **Phrases**
1. I am sure these mushrooms are **edible**. 2. The explorers were sure they would **starve**. 3. I am sure that was **deliberate**. 4. The divers soon found the **hull**. 5. The man shook a **fist** at me. 6. The tractor pushed the **boulder** away.
7. I began to **grope** in the dark room.
8. I put the **jewel** in the safe. 9. Bill took **enough**.
10. Last Saturday they were married in the **chapel**.

UNIT 20 **Sentence Structure**
1. b 2. b 3. b 4. a 5. b 6. b
7. b 8. b 9. b 10. a
Completed sentences will vary, but check for sense, capital letters and full stops.

UNIT 21 **Drawing Conclusions**
1. NF 2. F 3. NF 4. F 5. NF 6. NF
7. F 8. NF 9. F 10. NF 11. F 12. NF

UNIT 22 **Fact and Fantasy**
1. (a) fact (b) fantasy 2. (a) fantasy (b) fact
3. (a) fact (b) fantasy 4. (a) fact (b) fantasy
5. (a) fact (b) fantasy 6. (a) fantasy (b) fact
7. (a) fantasy (b) fact 8. (a) fact (b) fantasy
9. (a) fact (b) fantasy 10. (a) fact (b) fantasy
11. (a) fact (b) fantasy 12. (a) fact (b) fantasy

UNIT 23 **Comprehension**
1. a 2. b 3. a 4. b 5. b
6. a 7. c 8. b 9. b 10. b

UNIT 24 **Capital Letters & Full Stops**
1. It will be warm today.
2. The trees are losing their leaves.

3. Next January, the planet Venus will orbit close to the planet Mercury.
4. On the first Friday in July, Janet is going fishing in the Murray River.
5. The Darling River flows through New South Wales and Victoria and its waters eventually end up in South Australia.
6. Ashley and Mark are leaving next Tuesday.
7. John and I are going to Tasmania next July.
8. Tommy told me there was a serious accident in Wattle Street, Burwood, last Tuesday.
9. Colin Thiele wrote the books "Storm Boy" and "Sun on the Stubble".
10. The American film star Sam Smith, who lives in Los Angeles, visited Sydney last Christmas Day.

UNIT 25 Statements, Questions & Exclamations

1. Did you hear the train whistle blowing?
2. The wild horse bucked its rider off.
3. What a wonderful surprise!
4. When are Tom and Susan leaving to visit Vietnam?
5. You're always so happy!
6. Last Monday Chan and Wayne decided to hitchhike to Wagga Wagga.
7. Have you read "Storm Boy" by Colin Thiele?
8. You look gorgeous!
9. Why are the children who live in Maple Street always late for school?
10. How I wish you were here today!

UNIT 26 Statements, Questions & Exclamations

1. I am looking for Sally. Have you seen her?
2. What is the time? Shaun told me it was nearly eight o'clock.
3. Swan Hill is a large city in northern Victoria. It is well known for its farming.
4. What colour is a penguin? I think it is black and white.
5. How unlucky you are! Where did you lose it?
6. Who won the football match? I didn't hear the result.
7. What a beautiful day! Where will we go hiking?
8. Where is the best fishing spot? Is it over here in the deep water?
9. You're so smart! How did you think of that?
10. I see you won the first prize. Good luck to you!

UNIT 27 The Comma

1. Tom searched in the washing machine, in the sink, on the shelves, in the bath, and in the clothes basket, but couldn't find his singlet.
2. My best friends are Joel, Joshua, Sally, Paul and Chan.
3. Some large Australian cities are Sydney, Melbourne, Brisbane, Perth and Adelaide.
4. My best friend, Joshua, has been selected for the netball team.
5. The favourite sports of Jessica, my youngest sister, are cricket, netball, soccer, tennis and rounders.
6. In the river we caught cod, carp, bream, trout and catfish.
7. You expect your friends to come to your aid, but you never appreciate their help.
8. Our teacher, Mrs Jones, has been to England, Canada, Spain, France, China and Brazil.

UNIT 28 The Apostrophe of Contractions

1. didn't	2. can't	3. Let's	4. it's
5. We're	6. How's	7. isn't	8. won't
9. We've	10. aren't	11. I'll	12. couldn't

UNIT 29 The Apostrophe of Possession

1. dog's	2. girl's	3. elephants'
4. horses'	5. table's	6. trees'
7. men's	8. child's	9. children's
10. mouse's	11. bikes'	12. mice's

UNIT 30 Punctuation — Direct Speech

1. "When are we leaving?" asked Joe.
2. "Don't forget it is Paul's birthday tomorrow," whispered Sam.
3. "Where is Melbourne?" asked Susan.
4. "Is Perth the capital of Western Australia?" asked Sally.
5. "You look ridiculous in that dress!" sneered Josie.
6. "What a beautiful day!" exclaimed John.
7. "Is London the capital of England?" asked Clare.
8. "Why haven't you done your homework?" grumbled Mr Addison.
9. "I hope to be home by ten o'clock," said John, "If the tram is on time."
10. "I have done my best," I replied. "Aren't you satisfied with that?"

MASTERY TEST

1. flowers 2. fleet 3. John
4. (a) watches (b) thieves, cities (c) children, potatoes
5. brilliant 6. taller 7. Chinese
8. limped 9. buried 10. are
11. loudly 12. him 13. yet
14. between 15. (a) taught (b) saw
16. bald 17. (b) I read a newspaper each day.
18. (a) F (b) NF (c) F
19. (a) Next July, Clayton is going to England.
(b) When did Cassie go to Melbourne?
(c) I won! I am so surprised.
20. His brothers' names are Paul, Joe, Sam and Michael.
21. (a) isn't
22. the dog's claws, the tables' legs
23. "Where is my watch?" asked Sally.

THE FAMILY OF NAMING WORDS
NOUNS

Nouns are *naming words*. They are used to represent objects or persons such as dog, rock, lady, girl.

Which word best completes this list of nouns?
potato, tomato, carrot ____________
(a) cherry (b) bean (c) dentist
Answer = ***bean*** *as the other three in the list are also vegetables.*

Now do these.

1. bed, chair, table ____________
   (a) sofa (b) wall (c) roof

2. beef, pork, mutton ____________
   (a) giraffe (b) insect (c) veal

3. mouth, chin, eye ____________
   (a) nose (b) leg (c) cut

4. beetle, fly, ant ____________
   (a) cow (b) spider (c) butterfly

5. coat, singlet, shirt ____________
   (a) trousers (b) glass (c) book

6. cup, saucer, jug ____________
   (a) desk (b) knife (c) plate

7. train, car, bus ____________
   (a) calf (b) taxi (c) mutton

8. fever, cold, mumps ____________
   (a) measles (b) doctor (c) pens

9. valley, hill, mountain ____________
   (a) plain (b) engine (c) monkey

10. plane, hammer, saw ____________
    (a) chisel (b) bread (c) orange

11. butter, milk, cream ____________
    (a) cow (b) cheese (c) horse

12. liver, kidney, heart ____________
    (a) lung (b) doctor (c) hair

THE FAMILY OF NAMING WORDS
COLLECTIVE NOUNS

Collective nouns are names we use for *groups of things* or *groups of people*.

Example

Which noun best fills the gap?

The ____________ of birds is in the tree.

(a) hive (b) flock (c) set

Answer = (b). The ***flock*** *of birds is in the tree.*

Now complete these by choosing the best collective noun to fill the space.

1. There was a large ____________ at the concert.
(a) flock (b) herd (c) audience

2. We walked through the ____________ of apple trees.
(a) set (b) orchard (c) packs

3. Mrs Jones has a large ____________ of books.
(a) library (b) clump (c) crowd

4. There was a ____________ of warships in the harbour.
(a) team (b) fleet (c) crowd

5. Mike has a new ____________ of clothes.
(a) gang (b) pack (c) suit

6. A large ____________ of fish was seen in the bay.
(a) shoal (b) hire (c) case

7. She wore a ____________ of pearls around her neck.
(a) roll (b) string (c) tray

8. I put the ____________ of cards on the table.
(a) litter (b) pack (c) crew

9. There is a new ____________ of chickens in the yard.
(a) brood (b) carton (c) tribe

10. I bought a ____________ of eggs at the supermarket.
(a) box (b) carton (c) list

11. Our school has a large ____________ of teachers.
(a) staff (b) pair (c) case

12. Sally has a new ____________ of gloves.
(a) school (b) pair (c) litter

UNIT 3 THE FAMILY OF NAMING WORDS PROPER NOUNS YEAR 6

Proper nouns are words we use to name particular people, places and things. For example, *Joshua, Melbourne, Murray River, Wednesday*.

Proper nouns always begin with a **capital letter**.

Which word in each line is a proper noun?
Write it with a capital letter.
(a) flower (b) canada (c) book
Answer = **Canada**

Now do these the same way.

1. (a) friday (b) table (c) ink

____

2. (a) uncle (b) james (c) chair

____

3. (a) perth (b) pick (c) spider

____

4. (a) elephant (b) salad (c) july

____

5. (a) people (b) candy (c) norway

____

6. (a) christmas (b) theatre (c) city

____

7. (a) canary (b) yarra river (c) skeleton

____

8. (a) easter (b) dictionary (c) relation

____

9. (a) country (b) spencer street (c) king

____

10. (a) victoria (b) razor (c) engine

____

11. (a) mrs smith (b) mincer (c) violin

____

12. (a) capital (b) mazda (c) flower

____

13. Write the names of your two best friends.

________________ and ________________________

14. Write the name of your teacher. ______________________________

15. Write the name of the town or city in which you live. ______________________________

16. Write the name of the street in which you live.______________________________

17. Write the name of the closest river to your school. ______________________________

PLURAL NOUNS

Plural means *more than one*. Most nouns simply add -*s* to make their plural. For example, *one day — two days*.

Nouns ending in **-*ss***, **-*s***, **-*sh***, **-*ch*** and **-*x*** add **-*es*** to form their plural.
For example, *one hiss — two* ***hisses****, one peach — four* ***peaches***.

Example

Write the plural form of each word.
There are two ________ in the garden. (bush)
There are two ***bushes*** *in the garden.*

Now do these.

1. There are three ____________ in the garage. (bus)

2. I ate two ____________ for lunch. (apple)

3. Joan put all her ____________ on the bed. (dress)

4. There are three large ____________ in this street. (church)

5. The farmer shot over ten ____________ last night. (fox)

6. I put all the ____________ on the table. (box)

7. There are several ____________ in the cupboard. (brush)

8. Mike is wearing two ____________ today. (watch)

9. The good fairy gave her three ____________. (wish)

10. Our school has over twenty ____________. (class)

11. I put all the ____________ in the bin. (crust)

12. Several different ____________ make up our atmosphere. (gas)

PLURAL NOUNS

Plural means *more than one.*

Nouns ending in **-y** before which there is a **vowel** simply add **-s** to form their plural. If there is a consonant before the **-y**, then the **-y** is changed to **-i** and **-es** is added. For example, ***one monkey — two monkeys*** but ***one city — two cities***.

Most nouns ending in **-f** change the **-f** to **-v** and add **-es** to make their plural. For example, ***one loaf — two loaves***. Some nouns, though, simply add **-s**, for example, ***one hoof — two hoofs***.

If nouns end in **-fe**, the **-fe** is changed to **-v** and **-es** is added. For example, ***one life — three lives.***

Select the correct plural for each noun.
My dog has five ____________.
(a) puppys (b) puppies
*Answer = My dog has five **puppies**.*

Now do these.

1. There are three ____________ in the room.
   (a) babys (b) babies

2. I saw four ____________ in the paddock.
   (a) donkies (b) donkeys

3. All the ____________ have fallen off the tree.
   (a) leafs (b) leaves

4. There was a meeting of all the Indian ____________.
   (a) chieves (b) chiefs

5. There are four ____________ on the table.
   (a) knifes (b) knives

6. We have lots of ____________ in our kitchen.
   (a) shelfs (b) shelves

7. This cow has twin ____________.
   (a) calves (b) calfs

8. We picked all of the ____________.
   (a) cherries (b) cherrys

9. The ____________ were arrested by the police.
   (a) thiefs (b) thieves

10. Last night I made four ____________.
    (a) jellys (b) jellies

11. Last week I went to two birthday ____________.
    (a) partys (b) parties

12. The fairy story was about three ____________.
    (a) elfs (b) elves

PLURAL NOUNS

Plural means *more than one.*

(a) Nouns that end in **-o** have two ways of making their plurals. Some just add **-s**.
For example, *one piano — two* ***pianos***.
Others add **-es**. For example, *one potato — two* ***potatoes***.

(b) Nouns ending in ***-y*** with a consonant before the ***-y*** change the ***-y*** to ***-i*** and add **-es**.
For example, *one berry — ten* ***berries***.
Nouns that end in ***-y*** with a vowel before the ***-y*** simply add **-s** to make the plural.
For example, *one toy — two* ***toys***.

(c) Some nouns make their plural by changing a vowel or vowels or by adding ***-en***.
For example, *one man — two* ***men***.

Example

Write the plural of the word in brackets in the space.
I ate two ________ for lunch. (potato)
Answer = I ate two ***potatoes*** *for lunch.*

Now do these.

1. There are lots of ______________ in South America. (volcano)
2. The sheep were attacked by seven ______________. (dingo)
3. The five ______________ were on the lawn. (kangaroo)
4. I like to have lots of ______________ in my salad. (tomato)
5. We took lots of ______________ on the school camp. (photo)
6. There were lots of ______________ near the river. (mosquito)
7. There are many ______________ in our shed. (pliers)
8. The farmer has over one hundred ______________. (sheep)
9. We all like to wear ______________ to school. (jeans)
10. There are fifty ______________ on the farm. (goose)
11. I always clean my ______________ before going to bed. (tooth)
12. We caught over five ______________ in the traps. (mouse)

UNIT 7 THE FAMILY OF DESCRIBING WORDS ADJECTIVES YEAR 6

Adjectives are words that *tell us more* about nouns. They can describe *what kind, what colour* or *how many*.

For example, *It is a **large** dog. A ripe banana is **yellow**. There are **five** cars in the yard.*

Choose the best adjective to fill the space.
A knife that cuts well is ______________.
(a) blunt (b) sharp (c) loud
*Answer = A knife that cuts well is **sharp**.*

Now do these.

1. A deep pool is not ______________.
(a) wide (b) shallow (c) old

2. A bright light can be ______________.
(a) dull (b) silly (c) dazzling

3. The noise was ______________.
(a) deafening (b) blue (c) storming

4. I ate the ______________ meal.
(a) yellow (b) delicious (c) shallow

5. We ran away from the ______________ dog.
(a) savage (b) happy (c) purple

6. A ruby is ______________.
(a) red (b) hostile (c) brown

7. A tripod has ______________ legs.
(a) six (b) nine (c) three

8. The ghost story was quite ______________.
(a) kind (b) hollow (c) spooky

9. I enjoyed eating the ______________ meat.
(a) tender (b) sandy (c) noisy

10. It is a ______________ sky today.
(a) baggy (b) cloudy (c) empty

11. An angry person is ______________.
(a) hostile (b) happy (c) grey

12. A pentagon has ______________ sides.
(a) six (b) four (c) five

(a) When comparing **two** people or things, most adjectives add ***-er,*** and when comparing more than two, most adjectives add ***-est***.
For example, *My candle is* ***brighter*** *than yours.* (bright)
My candle is the ***brightest*** *of all.*

(b) If the adjective ends in ***-e***, this letter is dropped when adding ***-er*** or ***-est***.

(c) If the adjective ends in *-y*, change the *-y* to ***-i*** before adding ***-er*** or ***-est***.
For example, ***heavy*** ***heavier*** ***heaviest***.

(d) In some adjectives the last letter is doubled.
For example, ***hot*** ***hotter*** ***hottest***.

(e) In some adjectives, instead of adding ***-er*** or ***-est*** we add **more** or **most**.
For example, ***beautiful*** ***more beautiful*** ***most beautiful***.

(f) For some adjectives, the word is changed completely.
For example, ***good, better, best***.

Now, using the information above, write the correct form of the adjective in brackets.

1. Tom is the ______________ boy in the whole school. (small)
2. Beth is ______________ than her elder brother, James. (tall)
3. This is the ______________ apple on the tree. (large)
4. I think Jacob is ______________ than his cousin John. (wise)
5. Some of us feel Billy is the ______________ person in the school. (lucky)
6. Over here is much ______________ than where you are sitting. (safe)
7. This is the ______________ day we have had all year. (hot)
8. This pig is ______________ than that pig. (fat)
9. Julie is the ______________ girl in our grade. (honest)
10. I think pizzas are ______________ than hamburgers. (delicious)
11. I have ______________ lemonade than you. (little)
12. This is the ______________ day I have had all year. (bad)

PROPER ADJECTIVES

Some adjectives describe the people of a country.

Example

I like ________ wine. (Italy)
From Italy we can make the proper adjective, Italian.
*I like **Italian** wine.*

Like proper nouns, proper adjectives always begin with a capital letter.

Choose one of the proper adjectives from the box to fill the spaces below.

Spanish	Chinese	Dutch	Scottish	Welsh	Danish
Turkish	Swiss	French	Swedish	Mexican	Canadian

1. We ate some ______________ butter. (Denmark)

2. We saw some ______________ ponies trotting over the hill. (Wales)

3. My Dad likes to eat ______________ food. (France)

4. We bought some ______________ cheese at the supermarket. (Holland)

5. We ate some ______________ tacos for lunch. (Mexico)

6. This is a ______________ watch. (Switzerland)

7. Last night we dined at a ______________ restaurant. (China)

8. My uncle is in the ______________ Mounted Police. (Canada)

9. Over here are some ______________ carpets. (Turkey)

10. Last year we went for a holiday in the ______________ highlands. (Scotland)

11. Some ______________ dancers came to our school. (Spain)

12. A ship carrying ______________ timber docked yesterday. (Sweden)

THE FAMILY OF DOING WORDS — VERBS

Verbs are the most important words in sentences. They express an *action* being performed by a person or object. Every sentence must have at least one verb.

Example

Choose the best verb to fill the space.
The lady ________ to her dog.
(a) squeaked (b) called (c) bleated
Answer = The lady ***called*** *to her dog.*

Now do these.

1. The sun is ____________ brightly.
(a) running (b) shining (c) eating

2. We ____________ to win the match.
(a) hope (b) mope (c) play

3. The lame man ____________ down the street.
(a) ran (b) limped (c) darted

4. The duck ____________ across the lawn.
(a) waddled (b) lurched (c) staggered

5. The old flowers in the vase are

____________.
(a) hoping (b) laughing (c) fading

6. The detective carefully ____________ the fingerprints.
(a) snapped (b) studied (c) sighed

7. The dog ____________ at the stranger.
(a) laughed (b) cried (c) snarled

8. The rusty hinges ____________ as I opened the door.
(a) creaked (b) giggled (c) pleaded

9. When the child was drowning, the lifesaver

quickly ____________ into the water.
(a) leapt (b) played (c) wept

10. The injured lady ____________ from her wrecked car.
(a) staggered (b) replied (c) skipped

11. Dark clouds ____________ across the wintry sky.
(a) gathered (b) chuckled (c) played

12. The snake ____________ into a hole.
(a) jumped (b) gushed (c) slithered

VERBS — TENSE

Verbs that tell us about something that happened in the past are said to be in the past tense. Verbs make their *past tense* in different ways.

(a) Most add ***-ed***.
For example, *Today I* ***play****. Yesterday I* ***played****.*

(b) If the verb ends in **-e**, we drop this before adding ***-ed***.
For example, *Today I* ***arrive****. Yesterday I* ***arrived****.*

(c) Some verbs double their last letter.
For example, *Today I* ***beg****. Yesterday I* ***begged****.*

(d) If the verb ends in ***-y***, this is changed to ***-i*** before adding ***-ed***.
For example, *Today I* ***hurry****. Yesterday I* ***hurried****.*

(e) Instead of adding ***-ed***, some verbs change one or more letters.
For example, *Today I* ***ring****. Yesterday I* ***rang****.*

Now, by checking with the information above, add the past tense of the verb in brackets in the space.

1. Yesterday I ________ when I saw the snake. (scream)

2. When the teacher didn't hear me I _____________ my question. (repeat)

3. This morning we _____________ to leave for school early. (decide)

4. Billy _____________ a lot of time last week. (waste)

5. The lady _____________ the thief to the policeman. (describe)

6. Yesterday Anita _____________ all my spelling. (copy)

7. The boy ________ that he did not know the answer. (reply)

8. This afternoon the dog ________ the bone in the garden. (bury)

9. Last year we _____________ to England. (travel)

10. I couldn't sleep because the tap _____________ all night. (drip)

11. Our teacher _____________ us a song about a circus this morning. (teach)

12. Jenny _____________ a cricket bat for her birthday. (choose)

(a) The subject of a sentence must **agree** with its verb. If the subject is singular, the verb must also be singular. For example:
The boy ________ football well. (a) play (b) plays
"Boy" is singular so: *The boy* ***plays*** *football well.*
The girls ________ hamburgers. (a) like (b) likes
"Girls" is plural so: *The girls* ***like*** *hamburgers.*
Similarly, *The sun* ***is*** *shining. The stars* ***are*** *twinkling.*

(b) **Collective nouns** that are considered as a single thing take **singular verbs**.
For example, *The flock of birds ________ in the tree. (a) is (b) are*
The flock of birds ***is*** *in the tree.*

(c) Words denoting **sums of money** or **quantities** take a singular verb as they are considered single units. *For example, Fifty years* ***is*** *a long time.*

(d) If two nouns are joined by **and**, they take a plural verb.
For example, *Bill and Joe* ***are*** *coming along the road.*

(e) Some nouns that end in **-s** are really singular and take a singular verb.
For example, *Measles* ***is*** *a bad disease.*

Now, remembering the above, choose the correct verb for each of these.

1. The boys ____________ their work well.
(a) do (b) does

2. Mike ____________ to my home after school each day.
(a) come (b) comes

3. Lots of horses ____________ in the yard.
(a) is (b) are

4. Sally ____________ riding her bike down the street.
(a) was (b) were

5. Although she is only ten, Jill ____________ driven a car.
(a) has (b) have

6. Tom ____________ helping Susie do her homework.
(a) is (b) are

7. All the teachers ____________ going for a swim.
(a) was (b) were

8. The cows ____________ all been milked.
(a) has (b) have

9. A bunch of grapes ____________ in the bowl.
(a) is (b) are

10. A fleet of warships ____________ in the harbour.
(a) is (b) are

11. Ten dollars ____________ not a lot of money.
(a) is (b) are

12. I'm glad the news ____________ good.
(a) was (b) were

Adverbs are words that tell us more about the action of a verb. They usually tell us *how, when,* or *where,* something happened.

Bill ran **quickly.** (*How* fast did Bill run?) Sam will leave **tomorrow.** (*When* will Sam leave?)
Tom played **outside.** (*Where* did Tom play?)

Most **adverbs** end in *-ly*. In forming adverbs we often have to make spelling changes. For example;

(a) *quick,* ***quickly*** but *lucky,* ***luckily*** (we change the ***-y*** to ***-i*** before adding ***-ly***).

(b) If the word ends in **-e** we drop the **-e** before adding ***-ly***.
For example, *feeble* – ***feebly***.

(c) If the word ends in ***-l*** we simply add ***-ly***. For example, *thankful* – ***thankfully***.

Write the correct form of the adverb in the space.
We did the work ________. (easy)
Answer = We did the work ***easily****.*

Now do these.

1. The children sang ____________. (sweet)
2. The frightened horses galloped ____________ into the paddock. (quick)
3. The bus stopped ____________. (sudden)
4. Tom accepted the award ____________. (proud)
5. The dog barked ____________ at the children. (angry)
6. The kangaroo jumped over the fence ____________. (easy)
7. The children left the classroom ____________. (noisy)
8. The mother spoke ____________ to the small child. (gentle)
9. Sally behaved ____________ all day. (sensible)
10. The men carried the sheet of glass ____________. (careful)
11. We waited ____________ for news of the lost hiker. (hopeful)
12. Mike ____________ broke the classroom window. (accidental)

Pronouns are words which take the place of a noun.

For example, ***Sally*** *dropped the* ***ball*** *and the* ***ball*** *bounced back to* ***Sally****.*
This is clumsy to read. We can, however, replace **Sally** and **ball** with pronouns to make the sentence sound better: *Sally dropped the ball and* ***it*** *bounced back to* ***her****.*

Here are some common pronouns:
I you he she it we you they me him her them us

These pronouns show possession:
my our your his her its mine ours yours hers theirs

To find out whether to use **I** or **me** in a sentence, divide the sentence so that **I** or **me** is the only person in the sentence.

Bill and _____ are going to Perth.
You could not say ***Me*** *am going to Perth,* so it must be
Bill and I *are going to Perth.*
Similarly; *Dad told Bill and* ***me*** *to wait for him.*
That is, *Dad told Bill to wait for him; Dad told* ***me*** *to wait for him.*

Choose the correct pronoun to fill the spaces.

1. The dog chased ________ fast.
(a) us (b) its (c) he

2. Sam gave the ball back to ________.
(a) I (b) their (c) me

3. I saw the three boys as________ walked into the shop.
(a) he (b) they (c) them

4. The pens belong to me. The pens are

________.
(a) hers (b) mine (c) his

5. Sally and ________ are going to the movies.
(a) me (b) I (c) yours

6. This tent belongs to us. This tent is

________.
(a) ours (b) his (c) them

7. Tom skinned ________ knee when he fell down.
(a) him (b) he (c) his

8. That is ________ car in the garage.
(a) their (b) they (c) theirs

9. Please give all the marbles back to

________.
(a) they (b) them (c) he

10. The truck rolled down the hill

by ________.
(a) mine (b) itself (c) herself

11. Sam threw the ball to Sally and ________.
(a) me (b) I (c) their

12. This dog belongs to you. This dog is

________.
(a) him (b) yours (c) they

UNIT 15 THE FAMILY OF JOINING WORDS – CONJUNCTIONS YEAR 6

A *conjunction* is a word that joins together two single words or two groups of words.
For example, *salt **and** pepper.*

We will get wet. If it starts to rain. *We will get wet **if** it starts to rain.*

Some frequently used conjunctions are:

and if as but for yet that because since while
though unless whether although when until who

Choose the conjunction that best joins the sentences.
We must wait here ________ the bell rings.
(a) because (b) until (c) whether
*Answer = We must wait here **until** the bell rings.*

Now do these.

1. Sally cannot come ________ she is feeling ill.
(a) unless (b) but (c) because

2. ________ it heard the shot the rabbit raced into its burrow.
(a) When (b) Until (c) Who

3. We met a girl ________ comes from Tibet.
(a) that (b) who (c) because

4. ____________ I kicked five goals our team still lost.
(a) Although (b) When (c) Which

5. We will not rest ________ we have reached the top of that hill.
(a) until (b) because (c) whether

6. I cannot come with you ________ Mum gives me some more pocket money.
(a) who (b) that (c) unless

7. In our orchestra I play the violin ________ Joe plays the harp.
(a) because (b) and (c) who

8. ________ the girl fell off the swing, all the children were taken inside.
(a) Who (b) After (c) Yet

9. Mike had a sore leg ________ he still won the race.
(a) whether (b) but (c) for

10. Sally got into trouble ________ being late.
(a) until (b) and (c) for

11. I have not eaten any lollies ________ last week.
(a) although (b) since (c) yet

12. The farmer shot the dog ________ killed the chickens.
(a) who (b) that (c) when

UNIT 16 THE FAMILY OF PLACE WORDS – PREPOSITIONS YEAR 6

A preposition shows the *relationship* between a noun (or pronoun) and another word in the sentence.

For example, *Connor fell **down** the hill.*

'**Down**' shows us the relationship between Connor and the hill.

Some things to remember about prepositions are:

1. One thing is different **from** another – **not** different **to** or different **than**. For example, *My bike is different **from** yours.*
2. (a) **Into** shows movement **from** one place to another. For example, *She dived from the tree **into** the water.*
   (b) **In** shows position. For example, ***in** one place.*
3. **Beside** means **at the side of**. *The doctor stood **beside** the bed.* **Besides** mean in addition to – *Some girls **besides** Margaret were there.*
4. Something is divided **among** several people but **between** two people.

Now answer these by choosing the correct preposition.

1. We stayed inside the gymnasium ________ the storm.
   (a) for (b) off (c) during
2. I shared the lollies ________ John and me.
   (a) among (b) between (c) through
3. The barn is ________ the old house.
   (a) besides (b) beside (c) past
4. Sally jumped from the trampoline ________ the pool.
   (a) off (b) into (c) in
5. The teacher shared the cake ________ the whole grade.
   (a) between (b) among (c) to
6. My new pens are different ________ yours.
   (a) than (b) from (c) about
7. The boy hid ________ the bush.
   (a) behind (b) off (c) from
8. The cave was one hundred metres ________ the surface of the earth.
   (a) upon (b) under (c) past
9. The time is ________ six o'clock.
   (a) about (b) among (c) below
10. We get all our groceries ________ the supermarket.
    (a) near (b) of (c) from
11. Tomorrow is the tenth day ________ March.
    (a) off (b) of (c) from
12. The jet soared ________ the clouds.
    (a) from (b) except (c) above

CORRECT USAGE

Note the following:

(a) **Elder, eldest** are used for members of the same family.
Older, oldest are used for things or people not related.

(b) **Less, fewer** — **less** is used for quantities. **Fewer** is used for things that can be counted individually. For example, *I have **less water** than you. I have **fewer nails** than you.*

(c) **Hanged, hung** — a criminal is always **hanged** but pictures are **hung** on a wall.

(d) **Teach, learn** — remember a pupil **learns** but a teacher **teaches.**

(e) **Between, among** — things are shared **between** two people but **among** three people.

(f) As in Unit 12, a verb must agree with its subject.

Choose the correct word.

1. She ______________ coming tonight after all.
(a) ain't (b) isn't

2. I have ______________ sugar than you have.
(a) less (b) fewer

3. The coach said he'd ______________ me to kick a football.
(a) learn (b) teach

4. At school we ______________ how to spell correctly.
(a) learn (b) teach

5. Jason plays football ______________.
(a) good (b) well

6. There ______________ five books on the table.
(a) is (b) are

7. One of the horses ______________ tired.
(a) was (b) were

8. I have ______________ pencils than you have.
(a) less (b) fewer

9. This is the ______________ house in the street.
(a) oldest (b) eldest

10. Vanessa is the ______________ daughter of Mr and Mrs Morrison.
(a) oldest (b) eldest

11. The picture was ______________ on the wall.
(a) hung (b) hanged

12. The criminal was ______________ at the old convict gaol.
(a) hung (b) hanged

Sometimes we make errors when we speak or write.

Example

Choose the word that best fills the space.
Have you ever ________ a tiger?
(a) saw (b) seen
We need to choose the verb which agrees with the subject **you**, so the answer would be:
Have you ever ***seen*** *a tiger?*

Now do these.

1. Tom and I _______ going shopping.
(a) am (b) are

2. When my mother _______ home she cut the lawn.
(a) come (b) came

3. Sally _______ coming with us to the disco.
(a) ain't (b) isn't

4. I _______ a jet plane this morning.
(a) saw (b) see

5. Jack and Joe _______ going up the hill.
(a) was (b) were

6. ________ I have another piece of cake, please.
(a) Can (b) May

7. The balls ________ we bought were all flat.
(a) that (b) what

8. This morning was the first time Denise ________ to me since last week.
(a) speak (b) spoke

9. I just cannot walk ________ further.
(a) no (b) any

10. Mike ________ a bad accident yesterday.
(a) had (b) got

11. The window was ________ in the accident.
(a) broke (b) broken

12. The teacher was ________ angry with the silly girl.
(a) real (b) very

13. She plays netball ________.
(a) good (b) well

14. ________ girls are doing the work by ourselves.
(a) Us (b) We

A phrase is a group of words. Phrases can take the place of an adjective.
For example, *The man* ***with red hair*** *spoke to me (red-haired man)*
They can also replace an adverb. For example, *Jack fell* ***from the top of*** *the stairs. (down)*

Sometimes we use a phrase or several words when one word could be enough.

Circle the word that takes the place of the bold words.
The police soon caught the ***guilty person****.*
(camel, culprit, truant)
Answer = The police soon caught the culprit.

Now circle the word which would take the place of the bold words.
Write the sentence, replacing the phrase with the adjective.

1. I am sure these mushrooms are **fit to be eaten**.
   (sour edible stale)

   ____

   ____

2. The explorers were sure they would **die of hunger**.
   (starve delicious pray)

   ____

   ____

3. I am sure that was **done on purpose**.
   (frantic fatal deliberate)

   ____

   ____

4. The divers soon found the **body of the ship**.
   (hull box sail)

   ____

   ____

5. The man shook a **closed hand** at me.
   (knuckle fist arm)

   ____

   ____

6. The tractor pushed the **large rock** away.
   (pebble boulder puddle)

   ____

   ____

7. I began to **feel about blindly** in the dark room.
   (rush grope play)

   ____

   ____

8. I put the **precious stone** in the safe.
   (jewel watch cup)

   ____

   ____

9. Bill took **as much as he needed**.
   (little enough cheap)

   ____

   ____

10. Last Saturday they were married in the **small church**.
    (shop chapel garage)

    ____

    ____

UNIT 20 SENTENCES — SENTENCE STRUCTURE YEAR 6

A sentence is a group of words that expresses a complete thought — in other words it *must make sense.*

(a) At the football match.
(b) I saw Bill at the football match.

Example (a) is **not** a sentence because it does not express a complete thought by itself.
Example (b) does make sense by itself and is therefore a complete sentence.

Circle the complete sentence in each pair.
Rewrite the other group of words to make it a complete sentence.

1. (a) After seven o'clock.
(b) Cows eat grass.

2. (a) As the ice fell.
(b) I played while the rain was falling.

3. (a) Did you a dog?
(b) Where did Sam go?

4. (a) Sally is wearing a blue dress.
(b) Mike has a new.

5. (a) I threw a to my dog.
(b) My uncle took me to the footy.

6. (a) Georgina is learning her new bicycle.
(b) Adam threw the ball to me.

7. (a) On the road near the school.
(b) Sam plays soccer each Saturday.

8. (a) Why did you that flower?
(b) What is his name?

9. (a) As I was walking to school.
(b) Have you seen John?

10. (a) The horses galloped.
(b) Mike and I caught.

UNIT 21 — SENTENCES — YEAR 6
DRAWING CONCLUSIONS FROM GIVEN FACTS

When reading sentences we must be sure that the conclusions we draw are based on facts.

For example — *Sally is eighteen years old and has never seen snow.*

Look at these **conclusions** we could make about Sally.
(a) Sally is a teenager. (b) Sally is a girl. (c) Sally is blind.
(a) and (b) are based on **facts** given in the sentence. However (c) is not based on fact. There may be another reason that Sally has never seen snow. For example, she may have lived in a desert area all her life.

Read the statement above each column. Write "F" beside each conclusion based on fact and write "NF" beside those that are not based on a given fact.

(a) Last Saturday Emma and Joel, who are good friends, visited patients at the Royal Children's Hospital.

1. Emma and Joel are children. _____
2. They visited the hospital the day after Friday. _____
3. Emma and Joel visited the same patients. _____
4. Emma and Joel are good friends. _____
5. The patients had been injured in motor car accidents. _____
6. They went to the hospital at the same time. _____

(b) On that hot summer's day the two teenage boys were walking in the bush when one was bitten by a snake.

7. There were two boys walking in the bush. _____
8. The snake was a black one. _____
9. The boy was bitten by the snake in summer. _____
10. Two girls were also with the boys. _____
11. The boys were over 12 years of age. _____
12. The boy was bitten on the leg. _____

SENTENCES — FACT AND FANTASY

A fact is a *true statement*. You can prove that a fact is true. A fantasy is a *make-believe* idea.

Example

(a) Birds have feathers. **Fact**
(b) Birds like to read books. **Fantasy**

Read the pairs of sentences below. Write FACT beside those that state something factual and FANTASY beside those that are make-believe.

1. (a) Apples are delicious to eat. _______
(b) Cows like to cook bananas. _______

2. (a) Football is played with a square ball. _______
(b) Football is a popular sport in Australia. _______

3. (a) A dog is an animal. _______
(b) Dogs like to fly aeroplanes. _______

4. (a) Wheat and oats are both cereals. _______
(b) Horses love to go parachuting. _______

5. (a) An orange is a citrus fruit. _______
(b) Oranges chase butterflies in spring. _______

6. (a) Rabbits do their spelling homework each Monday. _______
(b) Rabbits are a pest of Australian farmers. _______

7. (a) Dogs wear yellow slippers to bed. _______
(b) Some dogs are used for guarding factories. _______

8. (a) Christmas Day is in December. _______
(b) A hen once wrote a book about Christmas. _______

9. (a) A lion is a type of large cat. _______
(b) Lions like to play cards. _______

10. (a) Books are an important source of information. _______
(b) Camels like to read books about water. _______

11. (a) Some birds build nests of sticks and twigs. _______
(b) Some birds go to school in buses. _______

12. (a) All insects have three body parts. _______
(b) Bees love to eat snakes and lizards. _______

Read this letter then circle the correct answer to each question.

Friday 7 March

Dear Sam,

I received your letter two days ago and I would like to wish you a Happy Birthday for next Thursday. My birthday is on the last day of the month and my mother's is two days before that.

I was glad to hear that you are going on holidays next Wednesday and will be in Brisbane on the 17th of this month. Next Monday our class is going to an excursion to the zoo. On 15 March I will be playing football against Maple Street Primary.

Yours sincerely,

Joshua.

1. What date is Sam's birthday?
(a) 13 March
(b) 21 March
(c) 15 March

2. What date is Joshua's birthday?
(a) 29 March
(b) 31 March
(c) 30 March

3. On what day did Josh receive Sam's letter?
(a) Wednesday
(b) Tuesday
(c) Thursday

4. On what date is Joshua's mother's birthday?
(a) 2 March
(b) 29 March
(c) 25 March

5. What day will it be on 15 March?
(a) Sunday
(b) Saturday
(c) Friday

6. On what date is the class going to the zoo?
(a) 10 March
(b) 11 March
(c) 12 March

7. What date is Sam going on holidays?
(a) 15 March
(b) 13 March
(c) 12 March

8. 17 March will be a
(a) Tuesday.
(b) Monday.
(c) Wednesday.

9. What day was it on 4 March?
(a) Thursday
(b) Tuesday
(c) Wednesday

10. What day was the first of this month?
(a) Sunday
(b) Saturday
(c) Tuesday

UNIT 24 PUNCTUATION CAPITAL LETTERS AND FULL STOPS YEAR 6

A statement always begins with a capital letter and ends with a full stop.

Example

i like to play football is punctuated –
I *like to play football****.***

Remember, also, proper nouns must begin with a capital letter.

I like to play football on saturdays. becomes –
I like to play football on ***S****aturdays.*

Rewrite the sentences, adding the capital letters and the full stops where they are needed.

1. it will be warm today

____

2. the trees are losing their leaves

____

3. next january the planet venus will orbit close to the planet mercury

____

____

4. on the first friday in july, janet is going fishing in the murray river

____

____

5. the darling river flows through new south wales and victoria and its waters eventually end up in south australia

____

____

____

6. ashley and mark are leaving next tuesday

____

7. john and i are going to tasmania next july

____

8. tommy told me there was a serious accident in wattle street, burwood, last tuesday

____

____

9. colin thiele wrote the books storm boy and sun on the stubble

____

____

10. the american film star sam smith, who lives in los angeles, visited sydney last christmas day

____

____

____

PUNCTUATION
STATEMENTS, QUESTIONS AND EXCLAMATIONS

A statement begins with a capital letter and ends with a full stop.
For example, *it is cold today* becomes ***I****t is cold today***.**

A **question** begins with a capital letter and ends with a **question mark (?).**
For example, *why is she crying* becomes ***W****hy is she crying***?**

Exclamations are sentences which express surprise.
An exclamation begins with a capital letter and ends with an **exclamation mark (!).**
For example, *what a lovely day* becomes ***W****hat a lovely day***!**

Exclamation marks can also express ridicule or sarcasm.
For example, *That was a great effort, you fool!*

Rewrite the sentences, adding the missing capital letters, full stops, question marks and exclamation marks.

1. did you hear the train whistle blowing

____

____

2. the wild horse bucked its rider off

____

____

3. what a wonderful surprise

____

4. when are tom and susan leaving to visit vietnam

____

____

5. you're always so happy

____

6. last monday chan and wayne decided to hitchhike to wagga wagga

____

____

7. have you read storm boy by colin thiele

____

____

8. you look gorgeous

____

9. why are the children who live in maple street always late for school

____

____

10. how I wish you were here today

____

____

PUNCTUATION
STATEMENTS, QUESTIONS AND EXCLAMATIONS

Remember:

Statements begin with a capital letter and end with a full stop. For example, ***I****t is nearly ten o'clock***.**

Questions begin with a capital letter and end with a question mark.
For example, ***W****hat time is it***?**

Exclamations begin with a capital letter and end with a exclamation mark.
For example, ***Y****ou're so smart***!**

Example

i have lost my watch have you seen it becomes –
I *have lost my watch*. ***H****ave you seen it***?**

In each activity there are two sentences. Punctuate each correctly.

1. i am looking for sally have you seen her

____

____

2. what is the time shaun told me it was nearly eight o'clock

____

____

3. swan hill is a large city in northern victoria it is well known for its farming

____

____

4. what colour is a penguin i think it is black and white

____

____

5. how unlucky you are where did you lose it

____

____

6. who won the football match i didn't hear the result

____

____

7. what a beautiful day where will we go hiking

____

____

8. where is the best fishing spot is it over here in the deep water

____

____

9. you're so smart how did you think of that

____

____

10. i see you won the first prize good luck to you

____

____

We use commas in a number of ways:

(a) To separate words in a list.
For example, *There were oranges, grapes, lemons and apricots on the farm.*

(b) To separate groups of words in a series. For example, *We looked under the table, on top of the shelf, beside the door but couldn't find the toy.*

(c) To separate where a reader should pause. For example, *You expect help, but you won't help me.*

(d) Commas are also used to separate words that stand for the same person or thing.
For example, *My sister, Juanita, likes to eat pizza.*
NB My sister and **Juanita** are the same person.

Rewrite each sentence, adding the missing commas as well as any other punctuation needed.

1. tom searched in the washing machine in the sink on the shelves in the bath and in the clothes basket but couldn't find his singlet

____

____

____

____

2. My best friends are joel joshua sally paul and chan.

____

____

3. Some large australian cities are sydney melbourne brisbane perth and adelaide

____

____

____

4. my best friend joshua has been selected for the netball team

____

____

____

5. the favourite sports of jessica my youngest sister are cricket netball soccer tennis and rounders

____

____

____

____

6. In the river we caught cod carp bream trout and catfish.

____

____

7. you expect your friends to come to your aid but you never appreciate their help.

____

____

____

8. our teacher mrs jones has been to england canada spain france china and brazil

____

____

____

THE APOSTROPHE FOR CONTRACTIONS

A contraction is a shortened form of two or more words.

Example

I ***do not*** *like eating turnips.*
I ***don't*** *like eating turnips.*

(Note the **-o** in "**not**" has been omitted and is replaced with an apostrophe.)

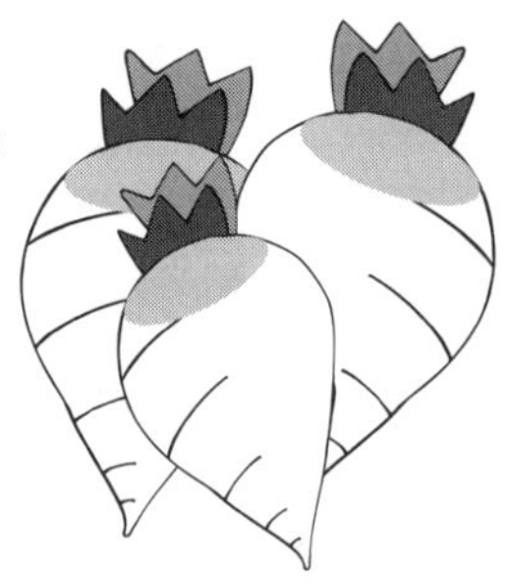

Write the contractions that can be formed from the underlined words. Don't forget to add the apostrophe where a letter has been omitted.

1. Mike **did not** come to the disco.

____

2. I **can not** help you unless you try harder.

____

3. "**Let us** sit over here," said Sally.

____

4. She told me **it is** nearly over.

____

5. "**We are** leaving soon," said Paul.

____

6. **How is** your brother going?

____

7. Mike **is not** ready to come with us.

____

8. We **will not** go fishing this weekend.

____

9. **We have** tried everything.

____

10. They **are not** allowed on the swing.

____

11. **I will** see you tomorrow.

____

12. Ahmed **could not** lift the heavy table.

____

UNIT 29 PUNCTUATION THE APOSTROPHE OF POSSESSION YEAR 6

The *apostrophe* can be used to show that a person or thing *owns* or *possesses* something.

1. The possessive of singular nouns is made by adding an apostrophe and then an **-s**.
   For example, *The bicycle of the* ***boy*** becomes *The* ***boy's*** *bicycle.*
   The hat of the ***lady*** becomes *The* ***lady's*** *hat.*

2. For plural nouns ending in **-s,** just add an apostrophe.
   For example, *The bicycles of the* ***boys****. – The* ***boys'*** *bicycles.*
   The hats of the ***ladies****. – The* ***ladies'*** *hats.*

3. For plural nouns not ending in **-s**, add an apostrophe and an **-s** (**'s**).
   Do not change the spelling of the original word.
   For example, *The pens of the* ***children*** *– The* ***children's*** *pens.*

Write the word and add the apostrophe in each (b) below. Use a red pen.

1. (a) the collar of the **dog**
   (b) the __________ collar

2. (a) the bicycle of the **girl**
   (b) the __________ bicycle

3. (a) the tusks of the **elephants**
   (b) the __________ tusks

4. (a) the foals of the **horses**
   (b) the __________ foals

5. (a) the legs of the **table**
   (b) the __________ legs

6. (a) the leaves of the **trees**
   (b) the __________ leaves

7. (a) the hats of the **men**
   (b) the __________ hats

8. (a) the toys of the **child**
   (b) the__________ toys

9. (a) the flags of the **children**
   (b) the __________ flags

10. (a) the whiskers of the **mouse**
    (b) the __________ whiskers

11. (a) the wheels of the **bikes**
    (b) the__________wheels

12. (a) the holes of the **mice**
    (b) the __________ holes

PUNCTUATION — DIRECT SPEECH

Quotation marks or inverted commas (" ") are used to show the actual words said by a person.

*Bill said **I will be home by six.***
The actual words Bill said are ***"I will be home by six"***,
so we enclose them in inverted commas.

Things to remember:

1. A comma is used to separate what is said from the rest of the sentence.
   For example, *"I am here," yelled Fred.*

2. Punctuation marks such as full stops, question marks and exclamation marks are always inside the inverted commas.
   For example, (a) *"Can we go soon"***?** (WRONG) (b) *"Can we go soon**?**"* (RIGHT)

Rewrite the sentences with inverted commas. Add any other punctuation needed. Use a red pen.

1. when are we leaving asked joe

   ____

   ____

2. don't forget it is pauls birthday tomorrow whispered sam

   ____

   ____

3. where is melbourne asked susan

   ____

   ____

4. is perth the capital of western australia asked sally

   ____

   ____

5. you look ridiculous in that dress sneered josie

   ____

   ____

6. what a beautiful day exclaimed john

   ____

   ____

7. is london the capital of england asked clare

   ____

   ____

8. why haven't you done your homework grumbled mr addison

   ____

   ____

9. i hope to be home by ten o'clock said john if the tram is on time

   ____

   ____

10. i have done my best i replied aren't you satisfied with that

    ____

    ____

MASTERY TEST YEAR 6

[ ] **denotes the unit to refer to.**

1. Which word is a noun? Underline it.
We picked the flowers carefully. **[1]**

2. Which word best fills the space?
I saw a _________ of ships in the harbour.
(flock fleet deck) **[2]**

3. Which word is a proper noun?
(a) west (b) pages (c) john **[3]**

4. Write the plurals of the words in brackets.
(a) We lost our _________ (watch) at the pool. **[4]**
(b) The two _________ (thief) worked in different _________ (city). **[5]**
(c) The _________ (child) didn't want to eat their _________ (potato). **[6]**

5. Underline the word which describes the light.
The brilliant light dazzled our eyes. **[7]**

6. Add the correct form of the word in brackets.
Mike is much _________ than me. (tall) **[8]**

7. Add the correct form of the proper adjective in brackets.
I like to eat _________ food. (China) **[9]**

8. Underline a word expressing action.
The injured boy limped slowly down the street. **[10]**

9. Use the correct form of the word in brackets.
Yesterday our dog ______ a bone in the backyard. (bury) **[11]**

10. Choose the correct word to fill the space.
The horses _______ in the stable. (is are) **[12]**

11. Which word tells how the baby cried?
The hungry baby cried loudly yesterday. **[13]**

12. Choose the correct word in the brackets.
Give it back to ________ now. (your him he) **[14]**

13. Which word best joins the two sentences?
We got up late. We still caught the bus.
We got up late _____ we still caught the bus.
(because yet until) **[15]**

14. Choose the correct word from the brackets.
The mushrooms were shared _______ the two girls. (among between from) **[16]**

15. Choose the correct word.
(a) My Mum _________ me how to plant trees. (learnt taught)
(b) I _______ some lovely buildings by the river. (seen saw) **[17, 18]**

16. What is the best word to replace the bold words?
He was **completely without hair** on his head. _________ **[19]**

17. Which of these is a complete sentence? ______
(a) Have you ever been?
(b) I read a newspaper each day.
(c) My dog loudly. **[20]**

18. Read the following sentence:
Last Tuesday we had soccer training at 3 pm instead of the normal time of 8 am.
From the information given, mark whether these sentences are fact (F) or non-fact (NF).
(a) Soccer training is usually held on a Tuesday. _________ **[21]**
(b) Soccer training was delayed because the field was flooded in jelly. _________ **[22]**
(c) Soccer training was held seven hours late. _________ **[23]**

19. Add the correct punctuation to each sentence below.
(a) next july clayton is going to england
(b) when did cassie go to melbourne
(c) i won i am so surprised **[24, 25, 26]**

20. Add the correct punctuation:
his brothers' names are paul joe sam and michael **[27]**

21. Write one word to replace the bold words.
John **is not** coming after all. **[28]**

22. Add the apostrophe in the correct place.
the claws of the dog — the dogs claws
the legs of the tables — the tables legs **[29]**

23. Add the quotation marks and any other punctuation needed.
where is my watch asked sally **[30]**

Notes

Notes

Notes